CW00522326

Marian Cox

Cambridge Checkpoint
English

Coursebook
9

CAMBRIDGE
UNIVERSITY PRESS

CAMBRIDGE
UNIVERSITY PRESS

University Printing House, Cambridge CB2 8BS, United Kingdom

Cambridge University Press is part of the University of Cambridge.

It furthers the University's mission by disseminating knowledge in the pursuit of education, learning and research at the highest international levels of excellence.

www.cambridge.org
Information on this title: www.cambridge.org/9781107667488

© Cambridge University Press 2014

First published 2014

Printed in the United Kingdom by Latimer Trend

A catalogue record for this publication is available from the British Library

ISBN 978-1-107-66748-8 Paperback

Contents

Introduction

Welcome to Cambridge Checkpoint English Stage 9.

The Cambridge Checkpoint English course covers the Cambridge Secondary 1 English framework and is divided into three stages: 7, 8 and 9. This book covers all you need to know for stage 9.

There are two more books in the series to cover stages 7 and 8, which have a different focus. Together they will give you a firm foundation in English.

During the year, your teacher may ask you to take a **Progression** test to find out how well you are doing. This book will help you to learn how to apply your knowledge of language and your skills in reading and writing in order to do well in the test. At the end of the year you will be asked to do a **Checkpoint** test to find out how much you have learnt over all three stages.

The framework's focus for stage 9 is **Argument and discussion**, and the study of persuasive and informative texts. The curriculum is presented in fiction and non-fiction content areas, and the skills are divided into Language (phonics, spelling and vocabulary, grammar and punctuation), Reading, Writing, and Speaking and Listening. There is no assessment of Speaking and Listening in the Progression tests or the Checkpoint test, but these skills, practised as individual, pair, group and class activities, are developed in all the units.

The topic for this book is **A world view**. The content is about viewpoints and opinions, and about how facts and ideas are presented.

This book has 12 units, each of which is a mixture of fiction and non-fiction passages and activities. There are no clear dividing lines between language and literature, or between reading and writing skills. Skills learnt in one unit are often applied in other units. There is, however, some progression in the order in which the skills are introduced, and you will be revisiting the skills practised in stage 7 and stage 8.

Each unit starts with an introduction which will prepare you for what you will learn in the unit, and a starter activity to get you thinking and talking. Each unit contains several kinds of passage and asks you to practise several skills. **Key points** explain rules and give information about aspects of reading and writing. **Tip** boxes provide help with specific activities. The activities are separated into stages to give you support. At the end of each unit you will be asked to do a piece of extended writing to give you the opportunity to practise the kind of writing you will be asked to do in the Checkpoint test. Other kinds of writing will be included in the activities. You will also practise reading the kinds of passage which are included in the Checkpoint test, and you will learn to read closely so that you notice the details of the content and of the language of what you read.

There are many different types of verse and prose in this book, and your knowledge of literature will be developed as well as your language skills. You will discuss ideas and methods with other students as well as with your teacher. These discussions are an important part of developing both your language skills and your understanding of literature. The contents list on page iii tells you what kinds of reading passage and writing activities occur in each unit.

We hope the course will be enjoyable and will help you to feel confident about responding to and using English in a variety of ways.

UNIT 1 Art, design and fashion

This unit focuses on argument and discursive writing. You will look at rhetorical devices, and also practise identifying reader positioning and analysing writers' stylistic effects. You will do some research, practise using colons and semi-colons and spelling, revisit summarising and sequencing, discuss a poem and write a magazine article.

Activities

1

a With a partner, list the names of as many artists or architects as you can think of.

b Now list the names of famous works of art or buildings.

c Write your own definitions for:
   i fashion
   ii architecture
   iii art.

Text 1A

What good is Art, and what is good Art?

What good is Art? This question is usually asked by tax-payers who don't think the state should 'waste' money on it, by parents who don't want their children to become artists because they don't see it as a secure career, or by governments who think universities should focus on science, maths and other 'useful' subjects which will benefit industry and the economy.

But did anyone ever ask what the work of Michelangelo and Leonardo da Vinci was good for? Our opinions about the need for the existence of art may have changed over the centuries. Those who defend it argue that Art (with a capital A) needs to exist because it makes people see, makes people think, or makes people happy.

But more to the point, what is good art? Where do we draw the line between art and non-art, and between good and bad art? And who decides? What kinds of creativity should be termed art? And what is the difference between an art and a craft? Who is worthy of being called an artist? And can it be a child or a monkey?

If art is used as advertising, for example on a box of chocolates or biscuits, does that demean it? And are the ridiculously high prices paid for a painting remotely justifiable? And should the public be denied access to national treasures kept hidden in exclusive private collections? And is abstract art as clever as representational art? One could go on and on asking questions about art, or Art.

2 In this activity you will look at the effect of the range of sentence structures used in Text 1A.

a Find examples of antithesis in Text 1A (i.e. words or phrases put together as opposites) and explain their effect.

b Find examples of balanced phrases in the passage (i.e. words or phrases with similar meanings) and explain their effect.

c Find examples of triple structures in the passage (i.e. the use of a grammatical form repeated three times in a row) and explain their effect.

3 Working in pairs, say what you notice about:

a the syntax (grammatical structures) in Text 1A

b the punctuation used in the passage

c the overall effect of the sentence types and use of punctuation in the passage.

Key point

Rhetorical devices

The use of questions not requiring answers is a rhetorical device used for persuasive effect. Being asked questions makes the audience/reader think about them and try to give an answer themselves. Rhetoric (the art of persuasive speaking or writing) began in ancient times when orators delivered speeches in public places to win support for a political view or course of action.

Here are some other rhetorical devices:
- deliberate repetition
- putting words in inverted commas or italics for emphasis
- antithesis and balance

- euphemism (making something sound more pleasant)
- juxtaposition (placing two ideas next to each other)
- rule of three (using three of a kind)
- bathos (ridiculous anti-climax)
- hyperbole (deliberate exaggeration)
- meiosis (understatement)
- tautology (another way of saying the same thing).

Breaking the normal rules of writing and starting sentences with *And*, *But*, *So* and *Or* also attracts attention and expresses an idea simply and directly enough to have an immediate emotional effect on the audience.

 a What do you think the writer's attitude to Art is in Text 1A, and what is the evidence?

b Make notes on your own views on Art, and think of some more questions you could ask about it.

c Using the devices mentioned in Activities 2 and 3, and using the passage as a model, write half a page about your views on the purpose and value of Art, and read it to the class in the style of delivering a speech.

Underwater wonder

The Mexican government has paid an artist to make 8,000 statues – all to be dumped on the sea bed. Why? In an attempt to save an endangered coral reef off the coast at Cancún, which suffers from repeated attack by hurricanes and is therefore at risk and needs protecting from anything which may further damage it. The statues of human figures now form the world's largest underwater sculpture display, 10 metres below the sea surface, which can be seen from boats passing above it. The statues are made from a specially hard and non-toxic form of clay. The first statues were lowered in 2006 and the site was declared open in 2009. The statues show human forms engaged in day-to-day activities, such as watching TV and driving a car. After being lowered to the sea bed, they are covered with coral to encourage growth. The aim is to tempt divers away from the

MesoAmerican or Manchones reef, the second longest coral chain in the world, to prevent further destruction to its delicate environment. There are now 500 statues, created and sunk over a period of 7 years by 38-year-old Jason deCaires Taylor, a British-Guyanese artist. It has been rated by National Geographic magazine as a contemporary Wonder of the World. The Cancún National Marine Park attracts 750,000 visitors annually. Taylor's target is to sink 8,000 statues in all; it will take several more years to achieve the conservation project. Not all the locals agree that this is a worthwhile endeavour, and some are concerned that it will attract even more divers to the area, many of whom are inexperienced. They believe that instead of protecting the environment, this artificial reef will actually damage it further.

5 Text 1B could be rearranged into a more concise and effective sequence.

   a **i** On a copy of Text 1B, add brackets to remove the repetitions and examples.

       ii Using numbers in the margin of the passage, decide on a new and logical order in which to use the material.

   b Rewrite the passage in a new sequence, linking ideas and using paragraphs.

   c After checking your work for accuracy and structure, give it to your teacher.

6 In this activity you will work in a small group to plan a presentation to the class.

   a Research the Seven Wonders of the Ancient World, and decide which one you think was the most spectacular.

   b Think of three sites you would wish to see on a list of contemporary man-made Wonders of the World, which may include one in your country.

   c Discuss and agree in your group which one is the most deserving of being on the list.

   d Make notes to explain what is so special about the site you have chosen.

   e One of the group presents your choice to the class, justifying why it deserves to be considered a Wonder. The class will vote on which sounds most impressive.

Text 1C

Giant shapes in the sand

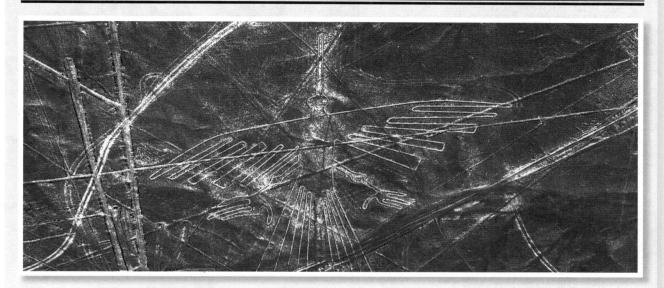

In the Nazca desert of southern Peru you can find the largest picture gallery in the world. But this is no ordinary display of art: the drawings, a whole **zoo** of animals and birds, are of monster size, laid out on the desert floor.

A giant condor has a wing-span of more than 120 metres; a lurking spider is nearly 50 metres long. There's a hummingbird with a **vast** bill, a curly-tailed monkey, a splashing whale, and many more birds, fishes and strange plant forms.

Because of their size, you can't really see the magnificent pictures at ground level. Only when airborne can you appreciate the whole wriggling, flying menagerie. They are highly stylised **outlines**, resembling the shapes which decorate the pottery of Indians who lived around Nazca from BCE to around 900 CE. They were made by the simple, if laborious, method of removing the dark stone layer which covers the desert, or *pampa*, and revealing the light-coloured sand beneath. The accuracy of the designs was probably achieved by skilful scaling-up of much smaller versions.

The awe-inspiring pictures were not discovered till 1941; they weren't easy to spot, since the desert winds had blown a thin dark layer of pebbles over the markings. The big puzzle is: why did Nazcas draw giant pictures in the sand which they couldn't see properly?

Perhaps they were for the gods, not humans, to see: most have connections in Nazca mythology with water, so they could have formed a kind of prayer for rain. Another theory is that the Nazcas gave their chieftains a burial ground that could be seen from the sky. It has also been argued that they had religious significance.

These **marvellous** monuments continue to **intrigue** and tantalise us; sadly, though, they are very fragile, and careless tourists have damaged a number of them. Now, the Peruvian government has banned everyone from the area where the best pictures are. Ironically, therefore, the world's biggest display of art can only be seen from the air, as originally intended but then lost sight of.

Hester Davenport, *Early Times*

7 a Find one or more synonyms in Text 1C for these five words in bold from the passage.

zoo   vast   outlines   marvellous   intrigue

b Why is there a question at the end of paragraph four?

c Look at the underlined phrase 'if laborious' and paraphrase it to show its meaning. Write a sentence of your own using 'if' in this way.

8 a On a copy of Text 1C, circle the colons. How many different types of usage for colons can you identify?

b How would you define the different uses?

c Write sentences of your own using colons in each of the different ways.

Key point

Colons (:)

The three functions of a colon are to:
- expand on or explain an idea (perform the function of *i.e.*)
- introduce items in a list
- introduce a quotation or significant piece of direct speech.

A colon does not need to be followed by a capital letter. Be careful not to confuse the colon with the semi-colon, which separates sentences and can take the place of a full stop, but which does not act in any of the ways listed above.

9 Now you are going to plan and write a summary of Text 1C.

a On a copy of Text 1C, underline the facts, and only the facts, about the Nazca sand pictures. (Do not include opinions, repetition, minor detail, comments, imagery or examples.)

b Transfer the underlined points to a plan, and decide on the order in which to use them and which ones to group together in the same sentence.

c Summarise the passage in as few sentences as possible, saving words by using semi-colons. Do not use more than 150 words (roughly half the length of Text 1C).

For Activity 9c
Semi-colons (;)

Semi-colons should not be overused in a piece of writing as they will make it seem list-like and lacking in fluency, because they add one simple sentence to another but do not help with the formation of complex sentences. They should be placed between closely related ideas only, and are used especially in informative types of writing requiring a concise style.

File   Edit   View   History   Bookmarks   Help

Kilroy was here

There are many versions of the legend <u>to explain</u> how the slogan 'Kilroy was here!' came to appear all over the world. The sentence started to be seen during the Second World War in places where US troops were stationed, and people still write it on walls to this day, <u>to continue</u> the joke. It is often accompanied by a drawing of a kind of fairy-tale figure looking over a wall. This famous image, known as 'Chad', consists of a face with two large oval eyes and a long nose, and two sets of three fingers holding onto a wall. The rest is hidden by the wall **itself**.

The best known explanation for the phenomenon is that there was a James J. Kilroy who was a ship inspector in the shipyard at Quincy, Massachusetts, USA. It was his responsibility <u>to check</u> on how many holes a riveter had filled during his work shift on any given day. <u>To prevent</u> double counting by dishonest riveters and <u>to prove</u> to his supervisors that he'd been doing his job, he began marking 'Kilroy was here' inside the hulls of the ships being built. He used yellow crayon so it would be easily visible; this way the other inspectors wouldn't count the rivets more than once and pay the riveter for work he hadn't done **himself**. (A female version of Kilroy, known as Rosie the Riveter, exists in some versions of the story.)

Once the ships became operational, carrying military troops that were headed overseas and bound for the war, it became a complete mystery why the phrase was still being seen, and not in ships but on buildings, and in out-of-the-way places. All anyone could be certain of was that Kilroy, whoever he was, had been there first. As a joke, troops began placing the graffiti **themselves** wherever US forces landed, claiming it had already been there when they'd arrived; it quickly became a challenge <u>to put</u> the picture and slogan in the most remote places before anyone else got there.

It is alleged <u>to exist</u> in the most unlikely places imaginable: on the top of Mount Everest in Nepal; on the torch of the Statue of Liberty in New York harbour; on the underside of the Arc de Triomphe in Paris; on the Marco Polo Bridge in China; on huts in Polynesia; and even scrawled in the dust on the moon.

10 Read Text 1D carefully and then work with a partner.

a Decide whether each of the following statements is true or false, according to Text 1D.
  i The Kilroy graffiti were originally found in places where there were American troops.
  ii The Kilroy graffiti date back to the beginning of the Second World War.
  iii The Kilroy graffiti started inside unfinished ships.
  iv US troops found the graffiti already there wherever they arrived.
  v It is unlikely that the Kilroy graffiti exist on the moon.

b i Look at the underlined infinitive verb forms in the passage. Decide which ones could have 'in order' placed in front of them to show intention.
  ii Rephrase the following quotation from the passage using 'in order to'.
  He used yellow crayon so it would be easily visible

c The words in bold in the passage are reflexive pronouns.
  i Agree on a rule for how this part of speech is used.
  ii Write other examples of sentences containing reflexive pronouns.

For Activity 10c
Reflexive pronouns

Reflexive pronouns, e.g. *itself*, have two different uses:
- to provide an object that is the same as the subject, e.g. 'I saw *myself* in the mirror'
- to refer back to and intensify a preceding noun, e.g. 'I saw the man *himself*'.

11
a Rewrite the first three sentences of paragraph two of Text 1D using different sentence structures. Begin in the same way: *The best known explanation for the phenomenon is …*

b Rewrite paragraph three as a summary. Make sure you include all the information.

c Look at the final paragraph of the passage. Write a sentence to explain its structure and its effect.

12
a If you wanted to leave a graffiti drawing, substituting your own name instead of 'Kilroy', what would your picture be of?

b Draw it on a piece of paper.

c Explain your choice of design to the class after drawing it on the board.

The next two activities focus on the vocabulary of Text 1E, including difficult spellings. Before you start, read the tip below.

For Activity 13c
Look Cover Write Check

This is one of the most effective methods for learning and correcting spellings:
- study the correct spelling of the word for a few seconds, taking note of its letter strings/sequences and 'hot spots'
- cover the word and write it according to the 'picture' of it you have in your mind
- check that your spelling of the word matches the original when you uncover it
- write the word correctly twice more, without looking at it, to fix it in your memory.

Text 1E

THE STREET RAT

Blek le Rat is a French street artist who calls himself 'The Man Who Walks Through Walls': he is a **phantom**, a shadow, a **myth**. He began his work as an urban decorator and political commentator in Paris in the early 1980s, when he was twenty. He is the **pioneer**, the ancestor, the grandfather of street art. He took to the streets when a Parisian fortune teller told him that she could see him working with walls. At first he misunderstood what she had meant: he started training to be an architect.

His real name is Xavier Prou, and at 56 years old he is far from being a youth **rebel**. He does not draw aggressive images, only reflective ones, and he says, 'My images are a present I make for everyone to enjoy, even children.' His dream is to be allowed to provide art to the city streets without having any problems. He was once caught by the police and the court case lasted a whole year. He then switched to putting up posters instead. They are faster; you cannot stay for longer than two minutes before the police come. And it's better for the walls.

His designs, based on life-size stencils of human beings and animals, don't decorate cities so much as haunt them. Their quirkiness, sarcasm and social observation make them poignant, humorous and political, like cartoon caricatures. His controversial career began with silhouettes of scampering rats, hence his name: that of a subversive city animal, but also an anagram of ART. These evil, thieving creatures of the night spread from Paris to the provincial French towns like a plague. He needed a secret identity because street artists, working under cover of darkness, obviously can't sign their real names for the police to trace.

He says that when you go on the street with a spray can, and spray your signature, you will go back and see it, because when you leave something in the street, you leave part of yourself. Street artists cannot resist coming back to admire their own handiwork; it is the main reason for doing it. He denies that he is a **vandal** or intends to destroy anything. He claims that the urge to produce graffiti, to fill a space on a blank wall, is a basic human instinct, and that it can never be stopped. You can trace it back to the decoration of cave walls 20,000 years ago. If a graffiti drawing is painted over, someone else will come and fill the gap.

Graffiti artists often have their own website to remind everyone of their 'works'. The internet has made street art a global movement, but it is the art of the common people and not of highly paid and respectable artists. There is no bigger contemporary cultural phenomenon in the world than street art. It is taking over the planet. Most cities are daubed with it, so much so that it is noticeable when there isn't any. You will see it in London, Rio, Melbourne, Barcelona, Beijing ... It is even being auctioned, like 'real' works of art.

13 a Write out the following ten words from Text 1E, which are useful but difficult to spell. Write them out with their 'hot spots' underlined.

architect   quirkiness   poignant   humorous   silhouettes
plague   contemporary   phenomenon   noticeable   auctioned

b Study the ten words, try to memorise their letter strings, and think of mnemonics to help you remember the silent letters and 'hot spots'.

c i With a partner, test each other on the spelling of the words.
ii Exchange responses to be marked out of ten. Make your corrections.

14 a Copy out the lists below in your notebook. Match the five words in bold in Text 1E with their meanings as used in the passage:
i phantom   person who resists authority
ii myth   wilful destroyer of property
iii pioneer   apparition
iv rebel   initiator
v vandal   fictitious person or thing

b Use these five words from the passage in a sentence for each which shows an understanding of their meaning:

phenomenon   controversial   quirkiness   subversive   poignant

c i Select ten words from the passage which have a strong negative connotation.
ii Explain to the class the reasons why these words are powerful.

15 Discuss the following as a class.

a In how many different ways are inverted commas used in Text 1E?

b Decide on five places where semi-colons could be used in the passage.

c i Why does the writer use a short sentence beginning with 'And' at the end of paragraph two of the passage?
ii What other forms of punctuation could have preceded it, other than a full stop?

16 a Using a copy of Text 1E, underline the words or phrases which make the reader sympathetic towards *Blek le Rat*.

b Explain how they achieve this effect.

c Now describe the activities of *Blek le Rat* as a statement of three sentences by a police officer, adopting an unsympathetic viewpoint.

17   **a** Discuss as a class the subject of graffiti and street art, and whether it is something that affects where you live.

      b As a class, collect points for and against street art. Write the points on the board in two columns, 'For' and 'Against'.

      c Using some of the points in the columns on the board, write two statements, one beginning 'Graffiti should be legal because ...' and another saying the opposite. Combine the points in a logical sequence in a complex sentence. Read out your arguments.

18 In small groups, read and discuss the poem in Text 1F. Make notes on the effect of the following to feed back to the class for discussion:

      a the punctuation

      b the layout and syntax

      c the rhyme and sound effects

      d the vocabulary and imagery

      e the message.

 Text 1F

maggie and milly and molly and may

maggie and milly and molly and may
went down to the beach (to play one day)

and maggie discovered a shell that sang
so sweetly she couldn't remember her troubles, and

milly befriended a stranded star
whose rays five languid fingers were;

and molly was chased by a horrible thing
which raced sideways while blowing bubbles; and
may came home with a smooth round stone
as small as a world and as large as alone.

For whatever we lose (like a you or a me)
it's always ourselves we find in the sea

e. e. cummings

DESIGN IDEAS THAT CHANGED THE WORLD

It is the simplest things that cause the greatest change. They are often harder to achieve than more complicated ones. Sometimes they are created by accident. We take them for granted when they become part of everyday life. We forget that someone, somewhere must have had the original inspiration for them.

Money

The barter system had its limits. If someone didn't want to exchange a product, to swap a chicken for a pot, what could you do? The answer was to use a token instead, so that trade could take place to the benefit of both parties. Money was introduced in China in around 200 BCE, the coins having a hole in the middle so that they could be strung together and worn around the neck. But they were heavy, so in the 9th century CE paper money was invented.

Bicycle

The first two-wheeled steerable machine appeared in Germany in 1817. It was made of wood and had no pedals, so it had to be moved by pushing one's feet against the ground. It was hard work, except for going downhill. Half a century later, a version with two equal-sized wheels and pedals was invented, which

immediately became popular with women as it gave them freedom to travel independently from the menfolk, who controlled the horse and buggy.

Flat-pack furniture

In the mid-1950s, a worker for a furniture company in Sweden couldn't get a new table into his vehicle, so he took the legs off in order to reassemble it when he got home. He realised that this was a breakthrough for the future making and selling of furniture, and presented the idea to his employers, IKEA.

Barcodes

The first barcode was made by extending downwards the dots and dashes of morse code to make narrow lines and wide lines out of them. This soon became a unique and universal method of cataloguing products as diverse as books and packaged food.

Velcro

A way of fastening two surfaces quickly but effectively by means of microscopic loops was the result of a dog-owner studying the way seeds got caught in his pet's fur when he took her out into the fields for a run, and the realisation of how difficult it was to remove them.

19 a Rewrite the five introductory sentences to Text 1G as two complex sentences. Express them in a more lively, discursive style. Read the key point below to help you.

b Think of five more designs that changed everyday life when they first appeared. Share your ideas with the class.

c Select one of your choices, and find out how it came to be invented. Then write a paragraph to explain its history, to accompany a picture of the item as part of a classroom wall display with the title 'Design ideas that changed the world'.

20 a Write a detailed half-page description of the outfit being modelled in the picture, as if for a fashion column in a magazine. Begin 'The latest craze to hit the catwalk is …'

b Survey five fellow students on their views about fashion, asking the following questions:
  i Does it exist just to make money for clothing designers and manufacturers?
  ii Does it have an unhealthy effect on models?
  iii Does it have too much influence on young people?
  iv Does it make society materialistic and competitive?
  v Does it affect the way you dress and the kinds of clothes you buy?

c Order the results of the survey in a plan for a discursive article titled 'Do we need Fashion?'

use b as a guide → **d** Write the article, of about one and a half pages, for your school magazine.

e **i** Exchange articles with a partner to check accuracy and clarity.
  ii Edit and improve it if necessary.
  iii Give your article to your teacher.

Key point

Discursive style and structure

Discursive writing aims to inform and also entertain. It presents a range of views without arguing for any particular one. The most common genre of discursive writing is the magazine or newspaper article (not a news report, which is very different). The style is lively and relaxed, sometimes humorous, and there is no fixed structure (unlike with argumentative writing) other than the presentation of each view separately, in its own paragraph, with details and examples to develop it. Unlike in purely informative writing, the first person can be used in places, and the writer may give their own opinion at the end.

UNIT 2 Modern living

Argumentative and persuasive writing are the focus of this unit. You will look at ways of making language effective and emphatic and the use of modal verbs, and practise paraphrasing, summarising and identifying topic sentences. You will argue a case, compare poems, and write an argument composition.

Activities

1 Consider these aspects of modern life.

a What kind of food do you eat, and what do you think about it?

b What kind of place do you live in, and what do you think about it?

c What do you think are the most concerning issues about life today?

Text 2A

A load of junk

One creature's rubbish is another's treasure. Nature has its own way of cleaning up – seagulls, cockroaches, rodents and flies carry off their spoil, and scavenging bacteria slowly break down even the hardest plastics. Human beings, unfortunately, are less dedicated to clearing up their waste.

Excessive consumption and rampant greed have caused the meaningless acquisitiveness of modern societies world-wide, and insufficient provision is made for what we do with the old and the empty. Fly-tipping is on the increase. Lorries drive at dead of night to abandoned industrial sites and remote beauty spots to dump mounds of rotting vegetables and builders' rubble rather than spend time and money on recycling it. Even more worryingly, chemical and medical waste is also being made to vanish in this way.

A rubbish dump twice the size of the United States has been discovered floating in the Pacific Ocean. It stretches from 500 nautical miles off the Californian coast, across the northern Pacific, past Hawaii and almost as far as Japan. The vast expanse of debris, made up of plastic junk including footballs, kayaks, Lego blocks and carrier bags, is kept together by swirling underwater currents. It takes a yacht a week to sail through it. Because the rubbish is translucent and lies just below the water's surface, it cannot be seen in satellite photographs. Cruise ships use the Caribbean as a rubbish bin.

Around a fifth of sea junk is thrown off ships or oil platforms – the rest comes from the land.

The rubbish island could double in size over the next decade if consumers do not cut back on their use of plastics. More than a million seabirds and 100,000 marine mammals die every year as a result of plastic pollution. Syringes, cigarette lighters and toothbrushes have all been found inside the stomachs of dead seabirds. This rubbish can also be dangerous for humans, because tiny plastic pellets in the sea can attract man-made chemicals which then enter the food chain when fish eat them. What goes into the ocean ends up on our dinner plate.

www.dailymail.co.uk

2 Work with a partner to summarise the news article in Text 2A.

a Give each of the four paragraphs an appropriate short heading to summarise its content.

b On a copy of Text 2A, underline the topic sentence or phrase in each paragraph (the key sentence or phrase indicating the subject).

c Reduce the passage to a one-paragraph summary of about 75 of your own words. Remember to leave out examples, figurative language, repetition, comment and unnecessary detail. One of you will read your summary to the class.

Text 2B

THE MODERN DIET

Children and teenagers like their food and drink fizzy, sweet and brightly coloured – and they want it now, now, now. They are notoriously reluctant to eat fresh fruit and vegetables – or indeed vegetables of any kind. Fizzy fruit was an experiment tried out a decade ago to try to tempt youngsters to eat fruit, but the carbon dioxide gas infused into it soon went out again, and the concept never caught on. A bright-orange drink aimed at young children, which made itself out to be no less than a health drink, lost its market when it emerged that the chemicals used to colour it were turning children yellow. Other tricks to overcome unwillingness to consume fresh produce have included 'snack-flavoured' vegetables, such as chocolate-flavoured carrots, baked-bean flavoured peas, and Brussels sprouts tasting of bubble gum!

The most consistent feature of the modern teenage diet is that it often consists largely or entirely of junk food, otherwise known as fast food. This has brought about international concern on many levels, from the personal to the political, from weight gain to global land use. The demands of international fast-food chains involve an ecologically damaging process which starts with deforestation and erosion in rural areas and ends with littering and packaging pollution on city streets.

There are campaigns to bring back slow food, traditional home-cooked dishes which take time to prepare and to cook – and to eat; such food was designed to be consumed in company, with the time to appreciate it, and the leisure to catch up with friends and family. <u>Not the least of</u> the arguments against fast food is that this form of nutrition – which is <u>far from</u> nutritious – makes us more rushed, more stressed and more isolated. This is because it can be eaten quickly, often actually on the move in the street or in a vehicle – and even bought in drive-through restaurants – and <u>more often than not</u> by someone eating alone.

Which brings up the question of what is in the fast food. There have been numerous scares and scandals in various countries about what manufacturers actually put in take-away meals and supermarket packets. The contents do not always match what it says on the tin, box or wrapper. This may be the result of deliberate deceit, because it was cheaper or easier to use another ingredient, or of accidental negligence which allowed something unhealthy or even poisonous to get into the production process. The cost to the company is then very serious, and for the victims it may be even worse …

3 You are going to look closely at the grammatical structures and stylistic devices in Text 2B.

a On a copy of Text 2B, underline the triple constructions (three of a kind) and write a comment to explain what you notice about the order of the three parts.

b Look at the underlined expressions in the passage and write a comment to explain the effect of these phrases.

c Collect a list of the balanced pairs of words (with *and* or *or* between them) in the passage, and write a comment to explain what you think their purpose is. Then read the key point below.

Key point

Binomial pairs

A binomial pair is an extreme form of collocation (i.e. words appearing habitually together) consisting of two adjectives, verbs or nouns, e.g. 'safe and sound'. These pairs of synonyms either begin with the same letter and/or repeat the same vowel sound (alliteration or assonance/rhyme). The effect of this tautology is to stress meaning by repeating it with another word.

Many binomial pairs are archaic – like 'hale and hearty', 'spick and span', 'kith and kin' – but have survived into modern usage because of the strength of their sound pattern, their familiarity in everyday usage, and the

fact that these 'identical twins' are inseparable and their order cannot be changed (for example we cannot say 'sweet and short' or 'sound and safe').

Antithetical pairs (opposites) balanced by *or*, such as 'trick or treat', 'thick or thin', 'sink or swim', are equally memorable for the same reasons; once again the order is fixed.

Although these are a form of cliché to be avoided in narrative writing, they can be effective in argument, where the aim is to persuade, which can be partly achieved through the appeal of familiarity.

d Comment on the use of 'from … to …' and 'starts with … ends with …' in paragraph two.

e Comment on the use of ellipsis (…) at the end of the passage. Then read the tip below.

For Activity 3
Devices for attracting attention

To win an argument or to get someone interested in reading a discursive piece, the writer has to find ways to first attract and then keep the reader's attention. There is no narrative to arouse curiosity, and the figurative descriptive language of an imaginative piece is not appropriate, so other devices have to be used to engage the reader. Noticeable features of language draw readers into enjoyment of the style of the writing, and they then become receptive to its content.

 a Deconstruct the second sentence in paragraph three, i.e. reduce it to the notes which would have existed before they were turned into phrases and clauses and then combined into one long complex sentence.

b Experiment with different ways in which to re-combine the notes into one complex sentence, using a range of punctuation and grammar devices.

c Swap with a partner, compare the different versions each of you were able to form, and decide which sounds the most persuasive and elegant.

For Activity 4b
More about sentence construction

You have already learnt various ways of forming varied and succinct sentences:

- by using a range of subordinating connectives (**not** *and*, *but*, *so*, or *or*)
- by using relative clauses, defining and non-defining (e.g. 'the boy, who was ill, didn't eat anything'; 'the boy who was ill didn't eat anything'; 'the table, which was too big, couldn't be used'; 'the table which was too big couldn't be used')
- by using present or past participle phrases, active or passive, with or without a preposition (e.g. *eating*, *having eaten*, *having been eaten*, *before eating*, *after having eaten*)
- by varying the order of clauses, for instance inserting a subordinate clause into a main clause (e.g. 'The visitors intended, since it was getting late, to go home as soon as possible.').

Now you can also practise forming sentences which include two interdependent ideas in an inseparable way:

a Using *that*, e.g. 'The girl was pleased that she had been invited to the party.' This is made up of two sentences which have been combined: 'The girl was pleased.' 'She had been invited to the party.' They are linked by reason, i.e. the girl was pleased *because* she had been invited to the party.

b Using *when*, e.g. 'The girl was pleased when she received an invitation to the party.' This is made up of two sentences which have been combined: 'The girl was pleased.' 'She received an invitation to the party.' They are linked by time, i.e. the girl was pleased *at the moment* she received an invitation to the party.

Try using different methods of sentence structuring, and changing the order of the phrases and clauses to make different versions of sentences, in order to give your style variety and to avoid starting them all the same way. Choose the construction that you think puts the emphasis in the most appropriate place, considering the content, purpose and style of the writing.

5 Now work with a partner to prepare speeches for a mini-debate on the subject of fast food.

  a **i** Collect points you would use to justify the need for the existence of fast food.

      ii Collect points you would use to persuade people to eat 'slow' food.

b Decide which side you will argue (your partner will take the opposite side), and organise your list of points into a speech lasting two minutes.

c Present your mini-debate to the class, who will vote on which side presented the most persuasive case in each pair.

At the risk of stating the obvious, raising teenagers isn't an easy job. The teenage years *may* be stressful and characterised by a considerable amount of screaming, crying, whining, and countless threats of running away from home – and that's just the parents. The teenagers generally engage in all of these attractive habits too, as they try to become independent creatures, straining on the leash of parental control, while parents try to cling on in order to protect their children, reluctant to let go and accept that their child is growing up.

Here are some tips for gaining respect and acceptance when dealing with teenage children:

- Don't make a fuss about nothing: if you do, your teen will not listen when it comes to the serious stuff. He or she will perfect the art of tuning you out if you relentlessly lecture them or punish them for trivial **infractions**. They are not interested in what is illegal, immoral, or even what is **detrimental** to their well-being, so it **can** be an uphill struggle to get them to take anything seriously.

- Offer options: doing deals **alleviates** the impression that you are controlling and that your teen is being controlled. Everyone needs to believe they have a choice and *can* make their own decisions – even if the right answer is inescapable. You have to allow them to feel they have some **autonomy**.

- Listen: you *can't* expect to be listened to if you discount their feelings and arguments without even considering them. You *may* not agree, but you should at least let them finish a sentence, and let them present their case before you dismiss it, to show that you are interested in their point of view and respect their judgement.

- Practise what you preach: if you are doing the opposite of what you are asking them to do, such as telling lies and being irresponsible, then you haven't got a leg to stand on. Teens **emulate** the people they respect and they need role models. You <u>must</u> admit your own failings rather than pretend you don't have any. They <u>need to</u> know that you are human too.
- Give reasons: always explain why they <u>have to</u> do something, rather than making it a case of 'Because I say so'. If they *can* see the logic behind your request then they <u>ought to</u> be more willing to do it.
- Deal with problems head on: there's no point tiptoeing around important issues. Be direct and open. Sugar-coating gives the impression you are afraid of tackling something and they will lose confidence in you, and *may* turn to someone else, someone less appropriate, for help.
- Stay involved: it's easy to switch off or keep your distance when you are disappointed, but teens need your support to help them withstand the enormous pressure from their peers. If you become remote your teen will feel alone, frightened and betrayed. If they are finding life difficult, they need your advice, even if they tell you the exact opposite, and you <u>ought to</u> be available for them.
- Enforce rules and discipline: if you don't lay down the law and teach your teen what the limits are, who will? They will always push to see how far they *can* go, and whether there are consequences to crossing the line. You <u>must</u> respond surely and swiftly when they <u>need to</u> be punished, because otherwise someone else in authority *might* be forced to do your job, like the headteacher or the police, and that **could** have disastrous and lasting effects well into adulthood.

6 In this activity you will look closely at the language of Text 2C, which is deliberately direct and provocative for the purpose of presenting argument.

a Give synonyms for the five words in bold in the passage. Then check your meanings in a dictionary or thesaurus.

infractions   detrimental   alleviates   autonomy   emulate

b In paragraph one of Text 2C:
 i find an example of understatement
 ii find a word being used ironically
 iii say where you would put an exclamation mark
 iv explain the effect of the dash and what follows
 v explain the sustained metaphor (one which continues rather than being used only once).

c On a copy of Text 2C find and underline as many examples as you can of figurative language (imagery) in the rest of the passage.

7 Work with a partner to investigate further the language of Text 2C.

   a Think of another way to express 'Sugar-coating' in Text 2C using non-figurative language. Which do you think is more effective, the original phrase or the replacement, and why?

   b Look at the use of the verbs *can/could* and *may/might*, in italics in the passage. Write an explanation of how each of these forms is used. Read the key point below if you need help.

   c Look at the use of the verbs *should, must, ought to, have to, need to,* underlined in the passage. Write an explanation of the rule for when each of these forms is used.

Key point

Modal verbs of probability and obligation

The modal verb *can* expresses ability, as in 'She can ride a bike', and *may* expresses permission, as in 'She may ride her bike'. This distinction is not always made nowadays, however, and *can* is often used for both meanings. The past tense forms *could* and *might* convey an increasing degree of uncertainty, e.g. 'She could ride her bike' (quite probable) and 'She might ride her bike' (possible but not probable).

   There are five other modal (auxiliary) verbs in English that refer to something to be done, with subtle differences and degrees of strength:
'He needs to agree' – necessity
'He must agree' – definite or imperative
'He has to agree' – predicts compliance; implies there will be consequences otherwise
'He ought to agree' – suggests a matter of duty
'He should agree' – expresses advisability or probability.

   Note that *must be* and *should* are not followed by *to*, but the other three modal verbs **are** followed by the infinitive form of the verb.

8 Now you are going to prepare a role play with a partner and perform it to the class.

   a Decide which of you will play the role of a parent and which the teenager. Then reread Text 2C, scanning for information which you can use in your role in an argument about how you see the relationship between parent and teenager.

b Make notes to remind you which ideas you will use when you perform your dialogue.

c Perform your role play to the class. Listen to and evaluate the other performances, taking into account the range of content and how well sequenced the dialogue is.

Cyberdanger

A cause for concern and anxiety has emerged with the **advent** and *prevalence* of the internet, cell phones and texting. The internet has exposed our children to a *potentially* sinister world, making them even more *vulnerable* and *accessible* to strangers than ever before. Even the kids who aren't looking for trouble find trouble looking for them on the World Wide Web. Without proper supervision and even *censorship*, the threats to teens are huge and ever increasing.

Often parents have no idea what their children are doing with their phones and computers in their bedrooms, because they spend no time with their children, are too busy using the same technology themselves, or have no idea how it works, what is out there in cyberland, and what it can lead to. Kids do not *volunteer* to tell their parents whom they are chatting to on the internet, so unless you ask you will never know.

It is a parent's job to ensure the safety of their children, and with the rapid **advances** in information and communications technology, the only way this can be achieved is with **vigilance.** You need to know which pictures they are uploading for the world to view, and what they themselves are viewing. Explain to your teens, and pre-teens, the dangers of providing personal information, either by instant message or as a post, to a favourite social networking site. A large majority of teenagers have created online **profiles** including photos of themselves. It is also common for them to post a picture of someone else which has caused the other person embarrassment, but which the victim is unable to remove and which may be used by others with *dubious* intent.

One in eight teenagers has given their mobile phone number online, and more than half of teens do not believe that posting photos and personal information on social networking sites is unsafe. They are wrong. Once their contact details are in the *system* they can be bullied, harassed or stalked. Twenty percent of teenagers have suffered from this. The data can be used to locate your child and to discover their *regular* routes and scheduled activities. Later, when they apply for a job, they must expect **prospective** employers to do a search to see what kind of pictures they have posted and what kind of comments they have made. What's done cannot be undone; even if it was done a long time ago, it is still used to judge *suitability*. There have been many cases of people losing their jobs because of the posting of inappropriate pictures of themselves or making unfortunate comments for all the world to see.

9 **a** Give synonyms, in the same part of speech, for the five words in bold in Text 2D:

advent   advances   vigilance   profiles   prospective

b Turn the following ten words, which are in italics in the passage, into other parts of speech.
prevalence ➔ verb
potentially ➔ noun
vulnerable ➔ noun
accessible ➔ verb
censorship ➔ adverb
volunteer ➔ adjective
dubious ➔ noun
system ➔ adjective
regular ➔ verb
suitability ➔ verb

c Look at the uses of *even* and *ever* in paragraph one of the passage and explain their effect.

10 Work with a partner for this activity, and make notes.

a Pick out the words which express powerful or controversial ideas in Text 2D.

b Pick out the three sentences that make clear the writer's views on this topic, and explain how you were able to identify them.

c Identify and write down three uses of persuasive or rhetorical devices mentioned in previous exercises in Unit 1 and in this unit (e.g. triple structures, antithesis, tautology).

d Comment on the kind of vocabulary and the kind of sentences that are used in this passage. Read the key point on the next page to help you.

Key point

Argument vocabulary and sentence types

The kind of vocabulary used in argumentative writing or speaking tends to be strong, extreme, even shocking. This attracts attention and evokes a response, giving a sense of urgency to the reader/listener. Even if the reader does not agree with what is being claimed, the provocative nature of the language will make it difficult for them to ignore the views being presented, and it may force them to engage in the debate. In Texts 2C and 2D there are many examples of words which are almost threatening in their connotations.

Another way of engaging or provoking a reader/listener is to make bold and categorical statements. They have the effect of suggesting that there is no possible doubt about the matter, that these ideas are facts and everyone agrees with them. Sometimes opinions are disguised in this way and the reader is manipulated by the assertiveness of the style into not questioning the claim. The sentences in argumentative writing tend to be simple or compound; this is so there will be no danger of the message being misunderstood.

e Using the material in the passage, make a list of 'Don'ts' as tips for your peers about using the internet. Read it out for the class to comment on.

The Planners

They plan. They build. All spaces are gridded,
filled with permutations of possibilities.
The buildings are in alignment with the roads
which meet at desired points
linked by bridges all hang
in the grace of mathematics.
They build and will not stop.
Even the sea draws back
and the skies surrender.

They erase the flaws,
the blemishes of the past, knock off
useless blocks with dental dexterity.
All gaps are plugged

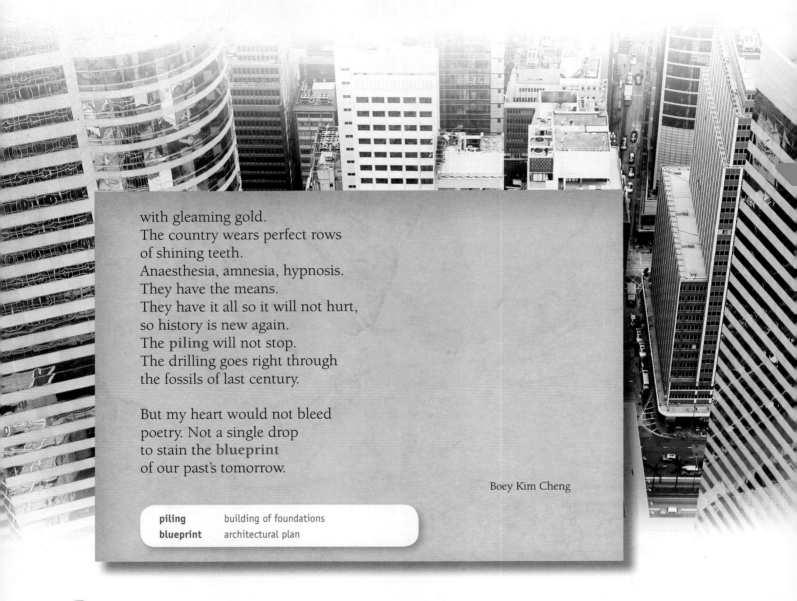

with gleaming gold.
The country wears perfect rows
of shining teeth.
Anaesthesia, amnesia, hypnosis.
They have the means.
They have it all so it will not hurt,
so history is new again.
The **piling** will not stop.
The drilling goes right through
the fossils of last century.

But my heart would not bleed
poetry. Not a single drop
to stain the **blueprint**
of our past's tomorrow.

Boey Kim Cheng

piling	building of foundations
blueprint	architectural plan

11 Discuss the following questions as a class after preparing notes with
a partner.

  a What is the sustained metaphor running through the poem?

  b What is the effect of the repeated references to 'They'?

  c What is the effect of the short run-on lines?

  d Which phrases stand out and why?

  e What do you think the last verse might mean?

Living off other people – Welfare

It would be pretty to have roses
Flourishing by my back door.
It would be nice to have a well-kept house
With velvet chairs not scraping a polished floor.
It would be lovely to sit down at dinner
Grey tie, pearl pin, fresh shirt and well-kept hands
And good to have a purring car in a clean garage
Eye-catching as the best brass bands.

But to keep it all going would be a lot of worry
And anyone who does it has to race and scurry
Seeing to roofs and pruning, maintenance and mechanics,
A shower of rain, a little green fly, bring on terrible panics
And ruin and failure shadow every path.

So I think this is the best thing to do:
As I walk down roads I see so many flowers
Nod-nodding in all the gardens that I pass.
I can glance into other people's rooms that they have furnished
And look how courteously that man is turning
To open the front door to his gleaming house.
Did you see how his suit fitted him, his perfect cuffs? Spotless cars
Slide by with women in furs and perfumes
Wafted to me with the flavour of cigars.

I am wrapped in my layers of shapeless coats
And I need never polish or dig or set
The table out for four distinguished guests
Or get to an office or prove myself each day
To provide for hammocks and lawns,
To get my antiques protected against insects.
A guest everywhere, I look in as dinner is served.
As I tramp past others' gardens, the rose opens.

Jenny Joseph

12 Discuss the following questions as a class after preparing notes with a partner.

a How does the narrator of Text 2F describe conventional suburban dwellers?

b What does the narrator in the poem feel about such lives and such people?

c i What is the narrator saying in the final stanza of the poem?
ii Think of a different title to match the message of the poem.

d The poem changes pace between slow and fast at various points. On a copy of Text 2F, write in the margin where you think this is happening. Can you explain the reason for the changes?

e What is the effect of the use of the following in the poem?
i occasional rhyme
ii different kinds of listing
iii run-on lines.

13 Write a comparison of the two poems Text 2E and Text 2F, of about one page, to give to your teacher. Consider the following aspects of the poems, and read the tip below to help you with the structure:

a Who is the speaker in each poem?

b What is the cultural context of each poem (i.e. how do they relate to modern living in terms of the society they describe)?

c What is the historical context of each poem (i.e. how do they relate to modern living in terms of the time period they describe)?

For Activity 13
Comparing texts

The clearest structure to use when comparing two texts is to:
- say in what ways the texts are similar, giving examples and quotations to support your views
- say in what ways the texts are different, giving examples and quotations to support your views
- say which one you prefer, and think is more effective, giving reasons for your judgement.

14

a Study the photograph of robots making cars. Write down your thoughts about this method of production.

b Add ideas about the way humans use computer technology in other aspects of modern life.

c Decide whether you wish to argue for or against the use of computer technology in the workplace, based on which side you have more points for.

d Organise your notes into for and against, and think about a good way to start an argumentative piece of writing with the title 'Computers: workers or bosses?'

e Write your argument composition, of about one and a half sides, using the key point below and the previous one to help you. Check your composition before giving it to your teacher.

Key point

Argument structure

Unlike discursive writing, an argument has to be carefully structured so that points against your case are presented first, and then dismissed, allowing the rest of the piece to concentrate on your own point of view, leading up to a strong conclusion. Showing you are aware of the other viewpoint at the beginning makes your case stronger, because it conveys that your opinion is not biased or unconsidered and can therefore be believed.

Your points – of which there should be several – need to be planned, put in order, and then supported to make them convincing. This support can take the form of a mixture of the following:

- statistics
- topical media stories
- factual background information
- examples
- quotations.

UNIT 3 Language and communication

This unit focuses on identifying and using key ideas, and considering different kinds of content and style in informative, argumentative and discursive writing. There is further vocabulary development and summary and spelling practice, and a look at discourse markers. You will write a letter to a newspaper, a blog post and a news report, and you will take part in a group discussion.

Activities

a What languages do you know, and in which situations do you speak them? When do you speak formally and when informally?

b What are your views about English as a global language?

c How often and in what ways do you rely on technology for your communications?

Technology revives the written word

Young people these days are **exposed** to an almost <u>constant stream</u> of the written word. They communicate by text messages (which now outnumber phone calls), or in internet chatrooms, or by Facebook updates (600,000 comments written every minute), or by tweets (340 million written per day).

When I was a lad, in the 1980s, we communicated by landline phone and we watched television. I never wrote a single word to anybody my own age, except perhaps to pass notes in class when I was bored. The internet and the mobile phone have changed all that, and put an **unprecedented** new emphasis on the written word, despite all the predictions that new technology would be <u>the death of it</u>.

Written words are important now. Everything, especially for the young, depends on them. Online chatting and searching, profiles and home pages, messaging and emailing, all depend on writing, and writing quickly. There is no time now for **pondering** the right phrase or planning the best way to say something before you make that phone call; that text and that mail demand an instant response. Communications have become shorter and more concise, more like **epigrams** than old-fashioned letters put in the post. Whether communications have actually become clearer and less **ambiguous**, or more subject to misunderstanding, is another matter.

The **essential** difference between writing and speaking is that writing can be crossed out, whereas speech cannot. Communication is now a continuous *work in progress*, as long as it's done on screen, and as long as you delete it before anyone reads it. *Which is just as well*, because instead of technology having made accuracy of spelling and grammar irrelevant, the move from the spoken to the written word has had the opposite effect: we judge accuracy severely, whether it be a romantic message or a job application, and are unimpressed by people who don't know how to use apostrophes or that definitely is spelt with an i.

Glancing around the internet, you can find examples of terrible English, but you'll also find an astonishing number of corrections.

There has probably never been a time in history when writing was so **universal** and so important. Books on the English language, even books on punctuation, can now *top the bestseller lists*. The **decay** of language and the disappearance of poetry and printed books – because of texting and tweeting – the self-love of Facebook, the rise of e-books, were **prophesied** until very recently, *but no more*. Words are **surging** around and across the world in an extraordinary, unstoppable blizzard, written and read on a scale that is quite mind-boggling. Today, the Philippines holds the record for texting: 27 per user per day. In Scandinavia, more than 85 per cent of the population communicates by text. Some 294 billion e-mail messages are sent every day, or 2.8 million per second. These are communications that until recently were made by telephone, letter, face to face – or, and this is highly significant in the communication debate, not at all.

The Sunday Times

2 Give synonyms for the ten words in bold as used in Text 3A:

exposed	unprecedented	pondering	epigrams	ambiguous
essential	universal	decay	prophesied	surging

3 Working with a partner, look at the following devices used in Text 3A and comment on their effects, i.e. what they contribute to a piece of argumentative writing:

a clichéd imagery (in italics)

b idioms (underlined)

c examples

d statistics

e subject pronouns.

4 Now consider the content of Text 3A with your partner.

a Summarise in one sentence the viewpoint of the writer on the subject of communication technology.

b Identify the arguments being used in Text 3A and list them.

c Give the counter-argument for as many of the items in your list as you can.

Text 3B

Language is forever changing

While teachers can be pretty sure that one and one will always make two, and that the capital of France will continue to be Paris, there's far less certainty when it comes to correcting English.

Language is like a stream. It moves on continually and, like a stream, will always take the easiest route. Any rule book about grammar is only ever going to be <u>a snapshot</u> of where our language is at the moment. If we look back to the dictionary which Samuel Johnson published in 1755, we see that words like 'wobble' and 'budge' were specifically excluded. As editor, Johnson considered both these verbs to be Americanisms which **replicated** perfectly adequate words already in English. 'Fun' was also disallowed for similar reasons. Eventually all three words <u>found their way into</u> English because, as the language moved forward, people discovered a need for them. Verbal communication will always be **pragmatic**.

Some words have undergone **fundamental** changes in meaning and **distinctions** have been lost. 'Nice', for instance, started off meaning 'foolish', then meant 'precise' and 'fussy', and now means 'vaguely agreeable'.

There is a very good argument these days for **rationalising** English, and making it <u>a level playing field</u> for everyone. Our young people struggle with the illogicalities of this language in a way that simply does not occur in Italian, Welsh or German, for instance. The simple rule of pronouncing whatever letters are in front of you seems to have **eluded** the English, which is why schoolchildren have such difficulty remembering to write 'through' rather than 'thru' and 'write' rather than 'rite'.

How much longer will the English stream <u>try to flow uphill?</u> In 1953 a bill actually came before the British Parliament for simplified spelling, but it failed. What governments can't manage is often left for the people to achieve. That is always <u>an ongoing process</u> with language, but at the moment QWERTY keyboard-driven technology and 'netlingo' is **accelerating** that process of simplifying and shortening, for example THX and F2F and CU for 'thanks' and 'face to face' and 'see you'. There is **minimal** or no capitalisation in textspeak, and onomatopoeic spelling, such as 'cooool'.

These forms may never be acceptable in an essay but, **ultimately**, any **innovation** within English that allows us to communicate unambiguously ought to be tolerated.

TES

- The skill is to be able to link what you want to say to what the previous speaker has said, either to agree and develop their line of argument, or to disagree and explain the reasons why you do not accept their viewpoint.
- There should be a sequence to the discussion so that the ideas are connected rather than a series of individual points.
- Listening to what others are saying is therefore very important, as well as a matter of courtesy, and you should not interrupt someone speaking. However much you disagree with a view, you should not be dismissive or mocking; everyone is entitled to have opinions and to express them.
- Ideas can be expressed as questions rather than always as statements; for instance you could say, 'I agree that most animals can't use human language, but what about the case of chimpanzees who have learned to use typewriters?'.

UNIT 4 Division and conflict

In this unit you will look at the role of argument in a range of prose, poetry and drama texts, and consider propaganda and satire. There is further practice in analysing and evaluating writers' effects and identifying reader positioning. The writing tasks include a diary entry and a newspaper editorial.

Activities

1 Work in pairs to prepare for class discussion on the topic of conflict.

a Agree on a definition for the word *conflict*.

b What are the causes of conflict? Give examples.

c What does conflict cause? Give examples.

Read the diary entries below, written by a girl called Zlata in Sarajevo, a city in the former Yugoslavia, during the Bosnian conflict.

Text 4A

> *Monday, 29 June, 1992*
> That's my life! The life of an innocent eleven-year-old schoolgirl!
> A schoolgirl without school, without the fun and excitement of school.
> A child without games, without friends, without the sun, without
> birds, without nature, without fruit, without chocolate or sweets,
> with just a little powdered milk. In short, a child without a childhood.
> A wartime child. I now realize that I am really living through a war,
> I am witnessing an ugly, disgusting war. I and thousands of other
> children in this town that is being destroyed, that is crying, weeping,
> seeking help, but getting none. Will this ever stop, will I ever be a
> schoolgirl again, will I ever enjoy my childhood again? I once heard
> that childhood is the most wonderful time of your life. And it is.
> I loved it, and now an ugly war is taking it all away from me.
>
> *Monday, 15 March, 1993*
> There are no trees to blossom and no birds, because the war has
> destroyed them as well. There is no sound of birds twittering in
> springtime. There aren't even any pigeons – the symbol of Sarajevo.
> No noisy children, no games. Even the children no longer seem like
> children. They've had their childhood taken away from them, and
> without that they can't be children. It's as if Sarajevo is slowly dying,
> disappearing. Life is disappearing. So how can I feel spring, when

spring is something that awakens life, and here there is no life, here everything seems to have died.

Saturday, 17 July, 1993
Suddenly, unexpectedly, someone is using the ugly powers of war, which horrify me, to try to pull and drag me away from the shores of peace, from the happiness of wonderful friendships, playing and love. I feel like a swimmer who was made to enter the cold water, against her will. I feel shocked, sad, unhappy and frightened and I wonder where they are forcing me to go, I wonder why they have taken away the peaceful and lovely shores of my childhood. I used to rejoice at each new day, because each was beautiful in its own way. I used to rejoice at the sun, at playing, at songs. In short, I enjoyed my childhood. I had no need of a better one. I have less and less strength to keep swimming in these cold waters. So take me back to the shores of my childhood, where I was warm, happy and content, like all the children whose childhood and the right to enjoy it are now being destroyed.

2 Work with a partner.

a Discuss and explain how the feeling of loss has been conveyed in Text 4A.

b Select and put into two columns the vocabulary used to convey the happiness of Zlata's life before the war and the unhappiness she feels now.

c How can you tell from the style that the diary entry was written by a child? List as much evidence as you can.

Text 4B is the former national anthem of Nigeria, used between 1960 and 1978; Text 4C is the current national anthem.

Nigeria We Hail Thee

Nigeria, we hail thee,
Our own dear native land,
Though tribe and tongue may differ,
In brotherhood we stand,
Nigerians all are proud to serve
Our sovereign motherland.

Our flag shall be a symbol,
That truth and justice reign,
In peace or battle honoured,
And this we count as gain,
To hand on to our children
A banner without stain.

O God of all creation,
Grant this our one request,
Help us to build a nation
Where no man is oppressed,
And so with peace and plenty
Nigeria may be blessed.

Lillian Jean Williams

Text 4C

Arise, O Compatriots

Arise, O compatriots,
Nigeria's call obey
To serve our Fatherland
With love and strength and faith.
The labour of our heroes past
Shall never be in vain,
To serve with heart and might
One nation bound in freedom, peace and unity.

O God of creation
Direct our noble cause
Guide our leaders right
Help our youth the truth to know
In love and honesty to grow
And living just and true
Great lofty heights attain
To build a nation where peace
And justice shall reign.

3 **a** Considering Text 4B and Text 4C, how would you define an anthem
and its purpose?

b How would you describe the form and content of the anthems?

c Summarise and paraphrase the message or argument of both anthems in one sentence each.

d How would you explain differences between the former and current versions?

e Which version do you prefer and why?

4 Work with a partner on this persuasive writing task.

a Think of a controversial cause, perhaps something to do with your country or your age group.

b Think of what you could say to persuade other people to support your cause.

c Write a paragraph to appeal strongly enough to readers to make them want to give their support. Read the key point first.

d Think of a slogan to be the heading for your paragraph.

e Read your piece to the class in a suitable voice.

Key point

Propaganda

The most biased form of argument is called propaganda, which is a text designed to serve the purposes of the writer as an instrument of persuasion within a conflict situation. Anthems are a form of propaganda because their purpose is political and their content is biased.

The devices used in this kind of persuasive writing are:

- assuming the reader is on the same side as the writer
- appealing to emotions of anger or pride
- keeping the claims very simple to grasp
- distorting or omitting facts
- telling half-truths
- exaggerating achievements
- using euphemism to disguise unpleasant ideas
- giving statistics to make claims seem valid
- calling the other side bad names
- using abstract positive words for the cause one supports
- repeating key words and ideas
- using simple syntax
- using a short, striking and memorable slogan similar to those used in advertising.

5 Look at the cartoon above and work in pairs to write a sentence for each of the following tasks, to be read out to the class.

a Describe what you see in the cartoon.

b Say what the cartoon shows about the apparent relationship between the characters.

c Say what it shows about their real relationship.

d Explain the difference between what the characters are saying and what they are thinking.

e Write a statement to explain the satirical message of the cartoon. Use the tip to help you.

For Activity 5e
Satire

Political cartoons, sometimes called caricatures, have the purpose of conveying a critical message about politics, either generally or in relation to particular politicians who are being satirised. Satire is the use of mockery to expose and attack vices such as foolishness, greed and hypocrisy in figures and institutions which have an effect on public life, e.g. parliament. Irony is the usual visual or verbal weapon used in satirical works, and satire can be amusing as well as shocking; the cartoon show *The Simpsons* is a good example of a satirical comedy in which every character represents a type of human who is being ridiculed.

Geography Lesson

When the jet sprang into the sky,
it was clear why the city
had developed the way it had,
seeing it scaled six inches to the mile.
There seemed an inevitability
about what on ground had looked haphazard,
unplanned and without style
when the jet sprang into the sky.

When the jet reached ten thousand feet,
it was clear why the country
had cities where rivers ran
and why the valleys were populated.
The logic of geography –
that land and water attracted man –
was clearly delineated
when the jet reached ten thousand feet.

When the jet rose six miles high,
it was clear that the earth was round
and that it had more sea than land.
But it was difficult to understand
that the men on the earth found
causes to hate each other, to build
walls across cities and to kill.
From that height, it was not clear why.

Zulfikar Ghose

6 Work in groups in preparation for class discussion.

a Say in what ways Text 4D is a poem.

b Comment on the structure and progression of the poem.

c If the poem were written out in sentences, as prose, what would be lost?

d What is the message or argument of the poem, in one sentence of your own words?

e What are the features of the poem which make it effective and memorable?

This passage from the novel *Lord of the Flies* shows the argument between the two rival leaders, Ralph and Jack. The conch is a large shell which anyone speaking at the meeting is supposed to hold.

Text 4E

There was a kind of sigh on the platform as if everyone knew what was coming. Jack's voice went up, **tremulous** yet determined, pushing against the uncooperative silence.

'He's like Piggy. He says things like Piggy. He isn't a proper chief.'

Jack clutched the conch to him.

'He's a coward himself.'

For a moment he paused and then went on.

'On top, when Roger and me went on—he stayed back.'

'I went too!'

'After.'

The two boys *glared* at each other through screens of hair.

'I went on too,' said Ralph, 'then I ran away. So did you.'

'Call me a coward then.'

Jack turned to the hunters.

'He's not a hunter. He'd never have got us meat. He isn't a prefect and we don't know anything about him. He just gives orders and expects people to obey for nothing. All this talk—'

'All this talk!' shouted Ralph. 'Talk, talk! Who wanted it? Who called the meeting?'

Jack turned, red in the face, his chin sunk back. He **glowered** up under his eyebrows.

'All right then,' he said in tones of deep meaning, and **menace**, 'all right.'

He held the conch against his chest with one hand and *stabbed* the air with his index finger.

'Who thinks Ralph oughtn't to be chief?'

He looked expectantly at the boys ranged round, who had frozen. Under the palms there was *deadly silence*.

'Hands up,' said Jack strongly, 'whoever wants Ralph not to be chief?'

The silence continued, breathless and heavy and full of shame. Slowly the red drained from Jack's cheeks, then came back with a *painful* rush. He licked his lips and turned his head at an angle, so that his gaze avoided the embarrassment of linking with another's eye.

'How many think—'

His voice tailed off. The hands that held the conch shook. He cleared his throat, and spoke loudly.

'All right then.'

He laid the conch with great care in the grass at his feet. The **humiliating** tears were running from the corner of each eye.

'I'm not going to play any longer. Not with you.'

Most of the boys were looking down now, at the grass or their feet. Jack cleared his throat again.

'I'm not going to be a part of Ralph's lot—'

He looked along the right-hand logs, numbering the hunters that had been a choir.

'I'm going off by myself. He can get his own meat. Anyone who wants to hunt when I do can come too.'

He **blundered** out of the triangle toward the drop to the white sand.

'Jack!'

Jack turned and looked back at Ralph. For a moment he paused and then cried out, high-pitched, enraged.

'—No!'

He leapt down from the platform and ran along the beach, paying no heed to the steady fall of his tears; and until he *dived* into the forest Ralph watched him.

William Golding

7 a What are the meanings and connotations of the five words in bold in Text 4E? Copy and complete the table below.

	Meaning	Connotation
tremulous	*shaking*	*nervously.*
glowered	*looking angrily*	
menace	*Threatin*	
humiliating	*Embarassing*	
blundered	*ran clumsily*	

b Comment on the effect of the five words or phrases in italics in the passage.

glared   stabbed   deadly silence   painful   dived

c Describe the atmosphere of the passage, and select words or phrases which create it.

8 a Choose quotations which show the character of Jack in Text 4E.

b Write a one-sentence summary for the character of Jack.

c Write a one-sentence summary to explain the source of conflict between Ralph and Jack.

9 Discuss the following as a class.

a What is the significance of the fact that Jack's choir have now become hunters?

b Which of the two characters do you think the reader is meant to sympathise with? Give reasons to support your answer.

c What does the reader expect to happen next, inferring from the clues which are given in the passage?

10 Imagine that you are either Ralph or Jack. Write your diary entry after the argument, referring to the following:

a what happened, including details and quoting speech

b how you feel about what you and your rival said and did

c what you foresee as the outcome of the conflict.

This poem is about the apartheid era in South Africa.

Nothing's Changed

Small round hard stones click
under my heels,
seeding grasses thrust
bearded seeds
into trouser cuffs, cans,
trodden on, crunch
in tall, purple-flowering,
amiable weeds.

District Six.
No board says it is:
but my feet know,
and my hands,
and the skin about my bones,
and the soft labouring of my lungs,
and the hot, white, inwards turning
anger of my eyes.

Brash with glass,
name flaring like a flag,
it squats
in the grass and weeds,
incipient Port Jackson trees:
new, up-market, haute cuisine,
guard at the gatepost,
whites only inn.

No sign says it is:
but we know where we belong.

I press my nose
to the clear panes, know,
before I see them, there will be
crushed ice white glass,
linen falls,
the single rose.

Down the road,
working man's cafe sells

bunny chows.
Take it with you, eat
it at a plastic table's top,
wipe your fingers on your jeans,
spit a little on the floor:
it's in the bone.

I back from the
glass,
boy again,
leaving small mean O
of small mean mouth.
Hands burn
for a stone, a bomb,
to shiver down the glass.
Nothing's changed.

Tatamkhulu Afrika

District Six	name of a former inner-city area of Cape Town in South Africa from which 60,000 non-white inhabitants were removed during the period of racial segregation in the 1970s
incipient	beginning to develop
Port Jackson	invasive, fast-growing willow tree with yellow flowers brought to South Africa from Australia, displacing the native species
bunny chow	South African fast food consisting of hollowed bread loaf filled with curry

11 Work in pairs to prepare for a class discussion on Text 4F.

a What is happening in the poem?

b Why is the speaker angry?

c What does 'we know where we belong' mean?

d What is the effect of the layout/short lines?

e What is the symbolism of:
  i the recurring image of glass?
  ii the reference to Port Jackson trees?

f What evidence does the speaker give to support his argument that 'Nothing's changed'?

g What is the effect of the last line of the poem?

h What is the effect of the use of historical present tense?

Key point

Historical present tense

Sometimes something that took place in the past is retold using the present tense, and this is called the historical or dramatic present to distinguish it from the real present tense. It is often used in colloquial narrative at the high point of the story (e.g. 'So then he goes back and looks for his friend ...'), and also in news reports in both the headline and for speech verbs. This gives the report more drama and immediacy than a past simple account, as well as reducing the number of letters.

In this scene from Act III of Shakespeare's play *Romeo and Juliet*, the feud between the two leading families of Verona in Italy comes to a head when Romeo and his friend Mercutio, who are <u>Montagues</u>, fight and kill the leading young <u>Capulet</u>, who is Romeo's relative now that he has just secretly married Juliet.

Text 4G

Enter ROMEO.

TYBALT	Well, peace be with you, sir: here comes my man.	
MERCUTIO	But I'll be hanged, sir, if he wear your livery.	
	<u>Marry,</u> go before to field, he'll be your follower;	
	Your worship in that sense may call him 'man'.	
TYBALT	Romeo, the hate I bear thee can afford	5
	No better term than this: thou art a villain.	
ROMEO	Tybalt, the reason that I have to love thee	
	Doth much excuse the appertaining rage	
	To such a greeting. Villain am I none;	
	Therefore farewell, I see thou knowest me not.	10
TYBALT	Boy, this shall not excuse the injuries	
	That thou hast done me, therefore turn and draw.	
ROMEO	I do protest I never injured thee,	
	But love thee better than thou canst devise,	
	Till thou shalt know the reason of my love;	15
	And so, good Capulet, which name I tender	
	As dearly as mine own, be satisfied.	
MERCUTIO	O calm, dishonourable, vile submission!	
	'Alla stoccata' carries it away. *[Draws his sword]*	
	Tybalt, you rat-catcher, will you walk?	20
TYBALT	What wouldst thou have with me?	

MERCUTIO	Good King of Cats, nothing but one of your
	nine lives that I mean to make bold withal, and
	as you shall use me hereafter, dry-beat the rest
	of the eight. Will you pluck your sword out of 25
	his pilcher by the ears? Make haste, lest mine be
	about your ears ere it be out.
TYBALT	I am for you. *[Drawing his sword]*
ROMEO	Gentle Mercutio, put thy rapier up.
MERCUTIO	Come, sir, your 'passado'. *[They fight.]* 30
ROMEO	Draw, Benvolio, beat down their weapons.
	Gentlemen, for shame forbear this outrage!
	Tybalt, Mercutio, the Prince expressly hath
	Forbid this bandying in Verona streets.
	[Romeo steps between them.]
	Hold, Tybalt! Good Mercutio! 35
	[Tybalt under Romeo's arm stabs Mercutio and flies
	with his followers]
MERCUTIO	I am hurt.
	A plague a' both houses! I am sped.
	Is he gone and hath nothing?
BENVOLIO	What, art thou hurt?
MERCUTIO	Ay, ay, a scratch, a scratch, marry, 'tis enough. 40
	Where is my page? Go, villain, fetch a surgeon.
	[Exit Page]
ROMEO	Courage, man, the hurt cannot be much.
MERCUTIO	No, 'tis not so deep as a well, nor so wide as a
	church-door; but 'tis enough, 'twill serve. Ask
	for me tomorrow, and you shall find me a grave 45
	man. I am peppered, I warrant, for this world.
	A plague a' both your houses! 'Zounds, a dog,
	a rat, a mouse, a cat, to scratch a man to death!
	a braggart, a rogue, a villain, that fights by the
	book of arithmetic. Why the devil came you 50
	between us? I was hurt under your arm.
ROMEO	I thought all for the best.
MERCUTIO	Help me into some house, Benvolio,
	Or I shall faint. A plague a' both your houses!
	They have made worms' meat of me: I have it, 55
	And soundly too. Your houses!
	Exit [with Benvolio]
ROMEO	This gentleman, the Prince's near ally,
	My very friend, hath got his mortal hurt
	In my behalf; my reputation stained
	With Tybalt's slander – Tybalt, that an hour 60

Hath been my cousin! O sweet Juliet,
Thy beauty hath made me effeminate,
And in my temper softened valour's steel!
[Enter Benvolio]

BENVOLIO   O Romeo, Romeo, brave Mercutio is dead.
That gallant spirit hath aspired the clouds,   65
Which too untimely here did scorn the earth.

ROMEO   This day's black fate on more days doth depend;
This but begins the woe others must end.
[Enter Tybalt]

BENVOLIO   Here comes the furious Tybalt back again.

ROMEO   Again, in triumph! and Mercutio slain?   70
Away to heaven, respective lenity,
And fire-eyed fury be my conduct now!
Now, Tybalt, take the 'villain' back again
That late thou gavest me; for Mercutio's soul
Is but a little way above our heads,   75
Staying for thine to keep him company:
Either thou or I, or both, must go with him.

TYBALT   Thou, wretched boy, that didst consort him here,
Shalt with him hence.

ROMEO   This shall determine that.   80
[They fight; Tybalt falls]

BENVOLIO   Romeo, away, be gone!
The citizens are up, and Tybalt slain.
Stand not amazed, the Prince will doom thee death,
If thou art taken. Hence be gone, away!

12 The scene can be acted out by the class – with four speaking parts and the rest of the students as supporters of the two sides. Then work in small groups on the following questions about Text 4G.

a Discuss any words you are not sure of the meaning of. Work out the rough meaning from their context and other similar words you do know.

b Which characters do you find sympathetic, and why?

c What do you notice about Mercutio's speech as compared to those of the other three speakers? Can you think of a reason for this?

For Activity 12c
Prose in Shakespeare

You have learnt that the plays of Shakespeare are mostly written in blank verse, which is unrhymed iambic pentameter (ten beats of alternately stressed syllables in a line). Occasionally, however, a character speaks in prose, even a noble one who normally speaks in verse. There is always a reason for this, to do with an extreme of emotion being felt by the character or a critical situation occurring in the play.

d What is Romeo saying in the couplet before Tybalt re-enters (lines 67–68)?

e After reading the tip below, find and list the examples in Text 4G of:
  i verbal irony
  ii situational irony
  iii dramatic irony.

For Activity 12e
Types of irony

The device of irony is a kind of division or conflict by definition, as it depends on the opposition of alternative meanings. Text 4G is an extract from a tragic play and tragedy usually involves irony, which introduces unfortunate misunderstandings. These make what happens more painful for the audience because we feel that it is just bad luck which causes things to go wrong, and that the tragic outcome could have been prevented.

Three types of irony may be used:
- verbal irony – when someone deliberately says the opposite of what they mean
- situational irony – when actions have the opposite effect from those intended, and when the outcome is unexpected, undesired or undeserved
- dramatic irony – when something is understood by the audience but not by one or more characters in the play.

13 Write one-paragraph character sketches, including quotations to support your interpretation, for:

a Romeo   b Mercutio   c Tybalt.

14 You are gathering information for a newspaper editorial on the recent tragic events in Verona.

a Write notes on what you would have witnessed as:
  i Benvolio (Romeo's cousin and Mercutio's friend)
  ii one of Tybalt's supporters.

b Make up a quotation to attribute to the Duke of Verona to show his attitude to the feud in his city, based on the evidence in the extract.

c Plan and write an editorial for the *Verona Herald*, with a title. It should comment on the fight and the deaths of Mercutio and Tybalt, and on the warring families and how the feud may develop. First read the tip below.

For Activity 14c
Writing an editorial

In a newspaper or magazine editorial, an editor not only gives a summary of a major recent news event but also comments on it, giving opinions which direct the reader to adopt the viewpoint of the owners of the newspaper and their political stance. It is therefore more of an argumentative than an informative piece, as the readers will already know about the event and will be looking for guidance as to how they should interpret it. The different sides of the case are explained and evaluated, but the editorial makes it clear which side it supports.

UNIT 5 Facing the future

This unit focuses on setting, pacing and structuring stories. You will look at style, collocations, character, suspense, prediction, and comparing stories with similar themes. You will write a review, plan a short story, and write a letter.

Activities

 1 Make notes on the following, for class discussion.

a What do you imagine your own future will be?

b What do you believe about the future of the planet?

c Suggest an item to be put in a time capsule to be opened in 50 years' time, and give reasons why it would be appropriate.

2012 is a futuristic disaster movie in which an American writer discovers that the world is about to end and travels from Los Angeles to China to try to save his son and daughter from the cataclysmic effects of climate change. Here are some of the comments made about it by film critics. Note that spelling and vocabulary are in American English.

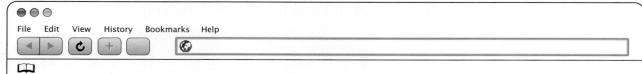

2012 features your pretty standard disaster movie requirements: an array of scientific nonsense, depictions of your favorite landmarks dying fiery deaths, and more people-escaping-in-the-nick-of-time sequences than is worth counting. There are three separate scenes with airplanes taking off from runways being consumed by fire! Three!

2012 is generally fun and has some unexpected twists in the story toward the end, so if you haven't seen a movie with lots of explosions and not much thinking this may fit the bill. Expect nothing intelligent about this movie and you'll be fine.

The camera is always high and dry to give audiences the best panoramic view, but it removes all tension from proceedings – you're always at a safe distance.

Two and a half hours of heaving and cleaving and crashing and crunching.

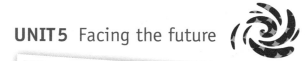

2012 is the rare case of a bad film that I'm nevertheless obliged to recommend you see.

Most of all, I liked the airlifting of giraffes to ark safety via helicopter and the bizarrely un-reasonable cheeriness of the beleaguered survivors who all but shout 'hip-hip-hooray' after billions of other Earth citizens lose their lives.

I can't claim to have seen every terrible film in cinematic history, but in my fairly extensive 'watchography', *2012* is certainly in the top five worst ever.

Gleefully over-the-top, this film takes the disaster movie pretty much as far as it can go.

Total popcorn entertainment with ridiculous dialogue and impossible situations and special effects that will boggle the brain for a good two-plus hours.

There's a whole world of destruction going on in the film's ridiculously excessive special-effects sequences. But there's a whole lot of entertaining going on, too.

My enthusiasm for *2012* is not because I think it's high art with an important social message. This movie is about pure spectacle, and it pulls that off fabulously.

Bigger, louder, crazier and more wildly exhilarating than anything previously attempted.

Films of this sort are plotted shish kebab style: disaster, change of scenery, new disaster. But on the level of spectacle, *2012* is top-notch.

A preposterous, overlong mess that's filled with cheesy dialogue and cliché-ridden characters.

Remarkably, *2012* doesn't even really try to be profound, which is a good thing. All it tries to do is what it knows how to do best: entertain. At that, it comes up a winner.

A deliriously ludicrous, guilty pleasure of a blockbuster in which the end of the world is turned into a two-and-a-half-hour rollercoaster ride.

It's easy to scoff at the over-reliance of CGI in contemporary cinema but for a film like this it's part and parcel of the whole, and computer-generated effects have never before been used as spectacularly.

www.rottentomatoes.com

2 Work with a partner on Activities 2 and 3.

  a What do the following colloquial words from Text 5A mean in formal language?

  over-the-top   boggle   top-notch   cheesy   blockbuster

  b List other metaphors and figurative expressions used in the comments.

  c Copy and complete the following collocations used in the comments, before looking to check if you are right.
     i nick of …
     ii at a safe …
     iii high and …
     iv hip hip …
     v part and …

Key point

Collocations

A collocation is a grouping of words, always in the same order, that habitually appear together and are remembered as whole phrases. They can be proverbs, clichés, traditional expressions, binomial pairs or fashionable terms, e.g. 'zero tolerance', 'once upon a time', 'green with jealousy'. They are more often found in speech than in writing, but are commonly used in argumentative writing, which relies on readers reacting positively to the language – and therefore to the ideas – that they find familiar.

3 You are going to write a review of the film *2012* using Text 5A.

  a With your partner, decide who will write the positive and who the negative review of the film, and select suitable material from the comments for whichever side you are on.

  b Organise your chosen material into a review, of about one page, using discourse markers and paragraph connectors. See the key point on the next page to help you.

  c Read your review to the class, in pairs, and they will decide whose recommendation to accept.

Key point

Writing a review

When reviewing a book or film you should first describe its genre, what it is about, where it is set, and who the main characters are. You can give a general plot outline but must not include the ending, as readers and viewers do not wish to know this in case they choose to read it or see it.

As with all types of argument, it will strengthen your case by making you seem less biased if you mention two or three things about the book or film which support the opposite view from the one you are presenting. Then go on to give your reasons for liking or not liking the work, with some supporting examples. End with a recommendation to either see/read the work or not.

Text 5B on the next page is the opening of a well-known futuristic novel called *1984* (published in 1949).

4 Work in a small group to collect notes for a class discussion.

a List all the evidence that Text 5B is set in the future.

b List the ways in which life in the future seems unsatisfactory.

c Copy the table below and complete it with the references made in the passage to the five senses.

sight	the telescreen
sound	The voice from the telescreen
smell	boiled cabbage, rag mats
touch	
taste	

d i Write a one-sentence summary of the setting of the novel opening.
  ii Explain the expectations created for the reader by the setting.

e i Discuss the connotations of the name Big Brother.
  ii Explain the implications of what we are told about him in Text 5B.

It was a bright cold day in April, and the clocks were striking thirteen. Winston Smith, his chin nuzzled into his breast in an effort to escape the vile wind, slipped quickly through the glass doors of Victory Mansions, though not quickly enough to prevent a swirl of gritty dust from entering along with him.

The hallway smelt of boiled cabbage and old rag mats. At one end of it a coloured poster, too large for indoor display, had been tacked to the wall. It depicted simply an enormous face, more than a metre wide: the face of a man of about forty-five, with a heavy black moustache and ruggedly handsome features. Winston made for the stairs. It was no use trying the lift. Even at the best of times it was seldom working, and at present the electric current was cut off during daylight hours. It was part of the economy drive in preparation for Hate Week. The flat was seven flights up, and Winston, who was thirty-nine and had a varicose ulcer above his right ankle, went slowly, resting several times on the way. On each landing, opposite the lift-shaft, the poster with the enormous face gazed from the wall. It was one of those pictures which are so contrived that the eyes follow you about when you move. BIG BROTHER IS WATCHING YOU, the caption beneath it ran.

Inside the flat a fruity voice was reading out a list of figures which had something to do with the production of iron. The voice came from an oblong metal plaque like a dulled mirror which formed part of the surface of the right-hand wall. Winston turned a switch and the voice sank somewhat, though the words were still distinguishable. The instrument (the telescreen, it was called) could be dimmed, but there was no way of shutting it off completely. He moved over to the window: a smallish, frail figure, the meagreness of his body merely emphasized by the blue overalls which were the uniform of the party. His hair was very fair, his face naturally sanguine, his skin roughened by coarse soap and blunt razor blades and the cold of the winter that had just ended.

Outside, even through the shut window-pane, the world looked cold. Down in the street little eddies of wind were whirling dust and torn paper into spirals, and though the sun was shining and the sky a harsh blue, there seemed to be no colour in anything, except the posters that were plastered everywhere. The black-moustachio'd face gazed down from every commanding corner. There was one on the house-front immediately opposite. BIG BROTHER IS WATCHING YOU, the caption said, while the dark eyes looked deep into Winston's own. Down at street level another poster, torn at one corner, flapped fitfully in the wind, alternately covering and uncovering the single word INGSOC. In the far distance a helicopter skimmed down between the roofs, hovered for an instant like a bluebottle, and darted away again with a curving flight. It was the police patrol, snooping into people's windows. The patrols did not matter, however. Only the Thought Police mattered.

Behind Winston's back the voice from the telescreen was still babbling away about iron and the overfulfilment of the Ninth Three-Year Plan. The telescreen received and transmitted simultaneously. Any sound that Winston made, above the level of a very low whisper, would be picked up by it. Moreover, so long as he remained within the field of vision which the metal plaque commanded, he could be seen as well as heard. You had to live – did live, from habit that became instinct – in the assumption that every sound you made was overheard, and, except in darkness, every movement scrutinised.

George Orwell

 a List the words and phrases from Text 5B which tell us about Winston Smith's way of life.

b Suggest what role he might play in the novel, based on what can be inferred from the passage.

c Write a paragraph description of Winston Smith, using supporting detail from the passage, bearing in mind that he is the anti-hero of the novel. The tip on the next page will help you.

For Activity 5c
Anti-heroes in literature

An anti-hero or -heroine is the main character in a work of modern fiction; they are flawed and lack traditional heroic qualities – such as courage, physical prowess or beauty – but they have enough good qualities to be sympathetic to the reader. They are usually helpless in a world over which they have no control, and are often seen as social outcasts because of their refusal or inability to conform. They have to struggle and endure in the course of the literary work, for which the reader admires them, but unlike a true hero they do not usually overcome enemies or succeed in their endeavours. This makes them more realistic and someone the reader can more readily identify with than a stereotypical classical heroic figure.

Text 5C is the opening of a futuristic short story called 'The Pedestrian', published in 1951.

Text 5C

To enter out into that silence that was the city at eight o'clock of a misty evening in November, to put your feet upon that buckling concrete walk, to step over grassy seams and make your way, hands in pockets, through the silences, that was what Mr Leonard Mead most dearly loved to do. He would stand upon the corner of an intersection and peer down long moonlit avenues of sidewalk in four directions, deciding which way to go, but it really made no difference; he was alone in this world of 2053 A.D., or as good as alone, and with a final decision made, a path selected, he would stride off, sending patterns of frosty air before him like the smoke of a cigar.

Sometimes he would walk for hours and miles and return only at midnight to his house. And on his way he would see the cottages and homes with their dark windows, and it was not unequal to walking through a graveyard where only the faintest glimmers of firefly light appeared in flickers behind the windows. Sudden gray phantoms seemed to manifest upon inner room walls where a curtain was still undrawn against the night, or there were whisperings and murmurs where a window in a tomb-like building was still open.

Mr Leonard Mead would pause, cock his head, listen, look, and march on, his feet making no noise on the lumpy walk. For long ago he had wisely changed to sneakers when strolling at night, because the dogs in intermittent squads would parallel his journey with barkings if he wore hard heels, and lights might click on and faces appear and an entire street be startled by the passing of a long figure, himself, in the early November evening.

Ray Bradbury

6   a   Write a one-sentence summary of the situation in Text 5C.

     b   Describe the setting of the passage and explain its effect.

     c   List the words and phrases which contribute to the atmosphere of the passage.

7   a   What is the effect of calling the character in Text 5C by his full name and title, Mr Leonard Mead?

     b   List the ironies in the passage.

     c   What do you think might happen next in the story, and what is your prediction based on?

8   a   What has happened in the future, according to Texts 5B and 5C?

     b   What do you think is the most worrying aspect of the future suggested by these stories?

     c   Write a half-page comparison of the two passages as futuristic story openings.

     d   Say which story you feel is more engaging and you would like to read more of, and why.

     e   Write your own opening to a futuristic story, of about a page, using ideas from both passages to help you:
         ● give details of the setting
         ● create an atmosphere and mood
         ● introduce the main character.

Text 5D is a complete short story called 'The Prisoner'.

Text 5D

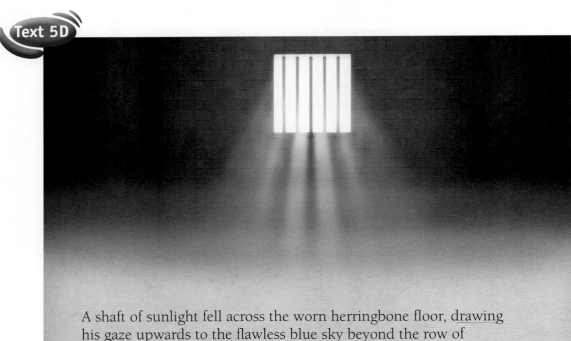

A shaft of sunlight fell across the worn herringbone floor, drawing his gaze upwards to the flawless blue sky beyond the row of windows, three metres above. It was a perfect summer's day. The kind of day, many years ago, when he might have taken the dog and run through the fields into the woods, climbed each of his favourite trees, and returned filthy and exhausted in time for tea. No thoughts of responsibility or duty. An **unfettered** spirit, in touch with himself and every other living thing. No clues to the future, to what he would, or would not, become.

He glanced left and right. They were watching him, expecting him to crumble, waiting for him to make a mistake. He daren't look behind to see how many more there were, mute and expressionless. A shudder ran through him.

His mouth was dry but he knew a drink was out of the question. Later, they'd smile apologetically, as though it were not their fault. As though it were **inevitable**; everything he'd done so far, leading to this.

He swallowed, licked his lips. Would he crack? Would he tell them what they wanted to know?

All the training, all the years of preparation, seemed worthless. He felt abandoned and defenceless in the face of what lay ahead and he clenched his teeth to prevent the last of his courage from escaping.

He thought about his family: his parents' pride and expectations. He was going to disappoint them, betray their trust. Even worse, he was going to let himself down.

He regretted all the time wasted on things he couldn't even recall. If he concentrated, if he could turn back time for a week, a month, a year, he could do it differently. Do it right. Tears pricked his eyes and he screwed them tightly shut, wishing it was a dream and he'd wake up, safe in his own bed, a carefree day stretching out before him.

How much longer? The waiting was torture in itself, calculated to **undermine** his confidence and shake the foundations of his knowledge. Sweat trickled down between his shoulder blades, prompting an **involuntary** twitch, and tension stretched his nerves until he expected an elastic snap as they gave way. It would come as a relief. Anything was better than this.

He studied the backs of his hands and **inhaled** deeply, forcing his shoulders down. He didn't want them to see he was already losing the battle. Flexing his fingers, he clasped his hands together, holding them between his knees in an effort to stop the trembling. He was as ready as he'd ever be.

The door behind him swished open and clicked shut. Precise footsteps clipped a path towards him, their echo mocking his weakness. He bowed his head and held his breath as they passed within inches before stopping. This was it. His vision blurred and panic clawed his guts.

A shrilling bell pierced the silence, followed by a brief, collective sigh.

'You may begin.'

He turned over his exam paper, picked up his pen, and began to write.

Susan Howe

9 Work in pairs on Activities 9 and 10 and feed back your answers to the class.

a Use the following words with prefixes from Text 5D in sentences of your own to illustrate their meaning:

unfettered   inevitable   undermine   involuntary   inhaled

b On a copy of Text 5D:
   i underline all the present participle phrases
   ii underline in a different colour all the examples you can find of non-sentences.

c There are very few adjectives and adverbs used in the story. Discuss the effect of this style.

For Activity 9c
Minimalist style

Minimalism is the name for any design or style, for example house furnishing and decorating, in which the simplest and fewest elements are used to create the maximum effect. In literature it means a style of writing which is stripped down to its essential components, i.e. nouns and verbs and grammatical lexis, without adjectives and adverbs. This economy of expression can give an impression of either dispassionate matter-of-factness – as if the writer isn't feeling any emotion or is keeping it suppressed – or of panic and lack of time to think properly or say anything more fully. It creates a fast pace and feeling of suspense in narrative writing.

10

   a Text 5D is deliberately ambiguous. Explain what the reader is led to believe and how.

   b When did you realise what the real setting and situation of the story are and why?

   c How much time do you think is covered by the story? What is the evidence?

   d How are tension and suspense created in the story?

   e What is the message or moral of the story?

11

   a Plan your own story about someone waiting nervously for something to happen.

   b Decide on a title.

   c Write some phrases and sentences you would include in your story to build tension.

   d Write a first sentence which sets the scene.

   e Write a last sentence to give a surprise ending, after reading the tip on the next page.

For Activity 11e
Plot twist endings

The most effective short story endings are those which use a narrative twist which is ironic or unexpected in some way. It must fit with what has gone before, however, so this is why it is very important to plan a narrative before you begin to write. You need to know in advance how it will end, and lay the clues from the beginning. Possible surprise endings are when a character turns out to be a different gender, age or even species from that which the reader was led to expect, or when characters do something drastic and unforeseeable because they have had enough of being mistreated and decide to rebel. It could be that the long-awaited and long-feared event turns out to be not as bad as expected, or that it doesn't actually ever happen.

Text 5E

Homes of the future

How will we live in the future? Are Star Trek fantasies of simulated-reality holodecks and revolutionary foodstuffs going to come true? We can suppose that many of the elements of what will be commonplace in a few decades, or even sooner, are already available to some consumers, or at least to researchers.

Key to much of our future lifestyle will be the use of resources. Imagining the home of the future is not simply about infusing more glamour into the places we live in today, and perhaps adorning the bathroom with LED lighting. What we can expect to see are devices that are not only more efficient than anything we have now but also provide greater connectivity between people and machines, allowing them to 'talk' seamlessly to each other.

It means an internet that is omnipresent. As Google's executive chairman Eric Schmidt put it, in the house of the future people are 'never

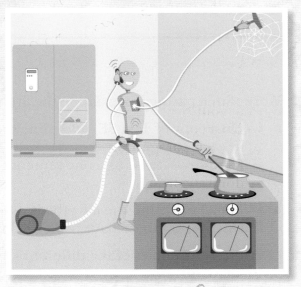

lost, never lonely, never bored'. He sees new technology as offering the possibility of 'a life of knowledge and entertainment – a potpourri for all of us to choose from'.

What would a visitor from the present day notice about the front drive of any house in 2020? If certain electronics companies have their way, it could be the charging plates for your electric vehicle. While wishful thinkers might say a glorified version of Skype video calling will make personalised transport redundant, the motor car is surely here to stay for a good while yet. Companies will still be around offering clever models for sharing cars, renting them and even turning them into automated taxis. Houses in smaller spaces will have had car turntables installed. And, of course, every lawnmower will be an autonomous 'robomower'!

Inside the house, the kitchen of the future is set to live up to the idea of eliminating tedious shopping. There are already fridge-freezers on the market that 'communicate' with other devices, as well as with retailers, to inform them what's inside. Via a screen on the door they can suggest what you might be able to cook with food that you have in the house, while providing advertisers with opportunities to recommend products. Some shops are already encouraging devices that automatically build up a shopping list and allow you to arrange 'one-touch' delivery.

The living room is the area that has seen the most profound changes in recent years, with personal video recorders altering our viewing habits and internet television allowing everyone to watch what they want, when they want. And with games consoles and smart TV a fixture in many houses, the idea of interacting with the television set is now established. Users of electronic games will already be familiar with the idea of just speaking to or waving at the television to make it do certain things; the idea is that rather than hunting around for the remote control, users can simply say 'pause' or wave – or even use a facial expression – to be able to browse through a list of programmes.

All of this is likely to be in an environment where everything – from thermostats to digital picture frames – is controlled by tablets or mobile phones, and such a high level of connectivity, much of it automated, should smooth out the tedium of managing a lot of gadgets. In the latest housing developments, that ubiquitous connectivity is built into the fabric of the building itself.

Matt Warman, *Daily Telegraph*

12 Work with a partner to examine the argument in Text 5E.

  a **i** On a copy of Text 5E, underline the topic phrase (the key idea) in each paragraph.
    ii Paraphrase these as a one-sentence summary to describe future domestic living.

  b **i** Put a box round the adverbials used in the passage.
    ii Discuss how these have been used to strengthen the argument.

  c **i** Circle examples of the different kinds of punctuation used in the passage.
    ii Discuss why these forms of punctuation are common features of argumentative writing.

13 **a** **i** The word 'omnipresent' is used in paragraph three of Text 5E. What does the prefix *omni* mean? Give examples of other words with this prefix.

ii Use the word 'ubiquitous' (penultimate line) in a sentence of your own to show understanding of its meaning.

  b The tense 'will have had' is used in paragraph four.
    i Try to work out what this tense is called by looking at the way it is formed.
    ii Give a rule for how it is used.

  c The word 'certain' is used in paragraphs four and six. Explain how the word is being used here in a different way from the other meaning of the word.

This letter was written by foreign correspondent Fergal Keane to his newborn son, Daniel.

Text 5F

Hong Kong, February 1996

My dear son, it is six o'clock in the morning on the island of Hong Kong. You are asleep cradled in my left arm and I am learning the art of one-handed typing. Your mother, more tired yet more happy than I've ever known her, is sound asleep in the room next door and there is a soft quiet in our apartment.

Since you've arrived, days have melted into night and back again and we are learning a new grammar, a long sentence whose punctuation marks are feeding and winding and nappy changing and these occasional moments of quiet.

When you're older we'll tell you that you were born in Britain's last Asian colony and that when we brought you home, the staff of our apartment block gathered to wish you well. 'It's a boy, so lucky, so lucky. We Chinese love boys,' they told us. One man said you were the first baby to be born in the block that year. This, he told us, was good Feng Shui, in other words a positive sign for the building and everyone who lived there.

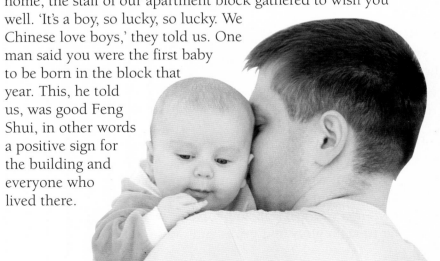

Naturally, your mother and I were only too happy to believe that. We had wanted you and waited for you, imagined you and dreamed about you, and now that you are here no dream can do justice to you. Outside the window, below us on the harbour, the ferries are ploughing back and forth to Kowloon. Millions are already up and moving about and the sun is slanting through the tower blocks and out on to the flat silver waters of the South China Sea. I can see the trail of a jet over Lamma Island and, somewhere out there, the last stars flickering towards the other side of the world.

We have called you Daniel Patrick but I've been told by my Chinese friends that you should have a Chinese name as well, and this glorious dawn sky makes me think we'll call you Son of the Eastern Star. So that later, when you and I are far from Asia, perhaps standing on a beach some evening, I can point at the sky and tell you of the Orient and the times and the people we knew there in the last years of the twentieth century.

Your coming has turned me upside down and inside out. So much that seemed essential to me has, in the past few days, taken on a different colour. Like many foreign correspondents I know, I have lived a life that, on occasion, has veered close to the edge: war zones, natural disasters, darkness in all its shapes and forms.

In a world of insecurity and ambition and ego, it's easy to be drawn in, to take chances with our lives, to believe that what we do and what people say about us is reason enough to gamble with death. Now, looking at your sleeping face, inches away from me, listening to your occasional sigh and gurgle, I wonder how I could have ever thought glory and prizes and praise were sweeter than life.

Daniel, my painful, haunting memories of suffering children I have come across on my journeys explain some of the fierce protectiveness I feel for you, the tenderness and the occasional moments of blind terror when I imagine anything happening to you. But there is something more, a story from long ago that I will tell you face to face, father to son, when you are older. It's a very personal story but it's part of the picture. It has to do with the long lines of blood and family, about our lives and how we can get lost in them and, if we're lucky, find our way out again into the sunlight.

When you are older, my son, you will learn about how complicated life becomes, how we can lose our way and how people get hurt inside and out. When my grandfather died, his son was too far away to hear his last words, his final breath, and all the things they might have wished to say to one another were left unspoken.

Yet now, Daniel, I must tell you that when you let out your first powerful cry in the delivery room of the Adventist Hospital and I became a father, I thought of your grandfather and, foolish though it may seem, hoped that in some way he could hear, across the infinity between the living and the dead, your proud statement of arrival. For if he could hear, he would recognise the distinct voice of family, the sound of hope and new beginnings that you and all your innocence and freshness have brought to the world.

 a Which of the following answers are correct in relation to Text 5F? Fergal Keane wrote this letter in order to:

   i express his feelings of pride and joy at having a newborn son

   ii express wonder and delight at how his life has changed as a result of becoming a father

   iii reflect on the world his newborn son has entered

   iv look back on his experience as a war reporter

   v express his wish that his dead father could know about the birth of his baby son.

  b **i** How would you describe the mood of the letter?

     ii Give examples of words which create this mood.

  c What is the structure of the letter? Give names to the different sections.

d i Identify the imagery used in the letter.
ii Explain why it is effective.

e Choose your favourite sentence from the letter, and explain why you find it moving.

15 You are going to write a similar kind of letter to the future, one which will be opened many years later by the person it is addressed to. This can be a real or imaginary person; if you wish, it can be your future self. Write between one and a half and two sides. Consider and plan the following aspects of the letter before you write it, check it, and give it to your teacher:

a the ideas, memories and hopes that you will include

b the setting and the mood of the letter

c the imagery which would be appropriate

d the overall structure

e the opening and ending.

UNIT 6 Making choices

This unit focuses on the role of choice in prose, poetry and drama. You will look at identifying opposing arguments and persuasive devices, and at distinguishing fact from opinion. There is practice in commenting on and comparing poems, writing an advertisement, providing an ending to a narrative, and writing a short story.

Activities

1

a List some of the major choices that you have made so far in your life.

b Contribute to a class discussion on the kinds of choices young people have to make, and give some of the items in your list as examples.

c In literature, making decisions is often compared to choosing which path to follow on the journey of life. Can you think of any poems, stories or films which use the metaphor of life being a road?

The poem in Text 6A uses American spelling.

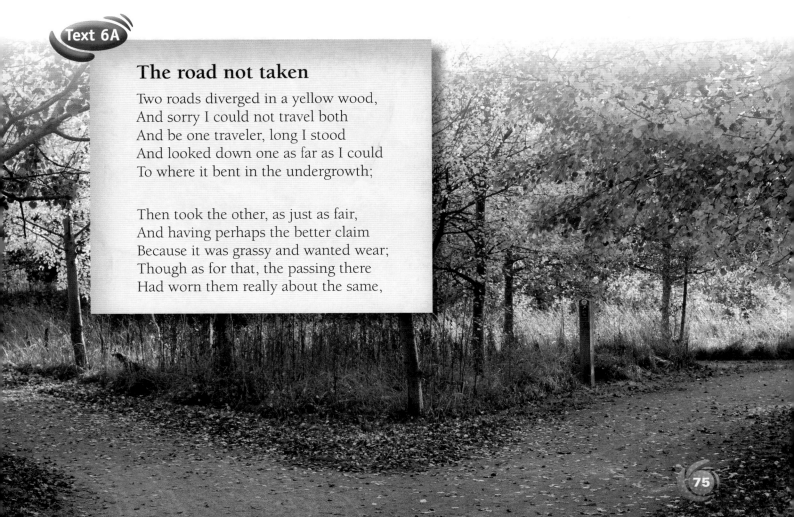

Text 6A

The road not taken

Two roads diverged in a yellow wood,
And sorry I could not travel both
And be one traveler, long I stood
And looked down one as far as I could
To where it bent in the undergrowth;

Then took the other, as just as fair,
And having perhaps the better claim
Because it was grassy and wanted wear;
Though as for that, the passing there
Had worn them really about the same,

And both that morning equally lay
In leaves no step had trodden black.
Oh, I marked the first for another day!
Yet knowing how way leads on to way
I doubted if I should ever come back.

I shall be telling this with a sigh
Somewhere ages and ages hence:
Two roads diverged in a wood, and I—
I took the one less traveled by,
And that has made all the difference.

Robert Frost

2 Work with a partner to prepare for a class discussion.

a There are ways in which this poem is regular, and ways in which it is irregular. Collect the evidence in two columns.

b Most of the words in the poem are monosyllabic, very few contain more than two syllables, and many of the lines begin with *And*. What effect is achieved by the use of such short and simple words?

c Notice how the first three verses are not really separate as there is only a semi-colon or comma between them, and many of the lines are run-on. What effect does this have on the poem, and why do you think there is a full-stop separating the third and final verses?

3 **a** Explain in your own words the meaning of the final verse.

b What is the persona really talking about in this poem? Describe it in one sentence after reading the key point below.

Key point

Allegory

The poem in Text 6A is allegorical, which means it is not really about someone walking in the woods but it has a deeper level of meaning. Many famous works of literature are allegories (like Aesop's fables), which are a kind of extended metaphor. The aim of an allegory is to make the reader infer the other meaning and the message being conveyed about an important aspect of human behaviour and existence. An allegory is a way of making a complex idea easier to understand, using simple everyday events and language.

c Do you agree that one should choose the road less travelled by? Work with a partner, one on each side, to collect ideas and supporting evidence for an argument on this topic, and perform it to the class.

Text 6B

Multiple choice

Many schools and colleges employ multiple-choice testing, not only for entrance tests but for end-of-course examinations. In some countries, such as the USA and former Soviet Union, such tests are **virtually** the only form of academic evaluation. But multiple-choice tests arouse dramatically differing opinions amongst supporters and critics; the former *swear by* them, while the latter are **resolutely** opposed.

Let's start with what is not disputed. A multiple-choice test is one in which the student is presented with a number of alternative answers – usually between three and five – and asked to select one – or more than one, according to the rules of the test – which answers the question. It is also agreed by all sides that these tests are easy to mark, as there is one acceptable answer, and no skill or judgement is required by an examiner. Indeed, many multiple-choice answer sheets are optically scanned and marked by computer.

It is for this latter reason that supporters describe these tests as 'objective' – the answer is simply right or wrong. It does not depend upon the ability of the student to express himself or herself clearly; it does not depend on how harsh or **lenient** the marker is; it is not subject to how tired the examiner is or their mood that day. Multiple-choice tests are therefore, say supporters, efficient and fair.

What of the critics? For them, almost everything about multiple-choice tests is anti-educational: they **stifle** initiative and force students to think alike; they encourage closed minds; they *foster the fallacy* that there is always a right answer, and only one right answer, to life's

questions. Critics **scoff** at the idea that true understanding and subtle appreciation can be tested in this way, and ridicule the simplicity of multiple-choice questions with such examples as 'Was Shakespeare a great writer? Yes/No/ Maybe.' They also, more **tellingly**, point out that so-called 'distractor' answers, the wrong ones, can mislead **unwary** candidates, and they claim that students who have been **coached** in multiple-choice techniques do better in the exam, regardless of their actual level of knowledge, than those who have not.

Research has proved that a candidate will inevitably score 20% if there are five answers, and 33% if there are only three, by simply circling answer 'A' every time. **Fundamentally**, critics say, these tests *give the illusion of* objectivity only because it is easy to count whether the candidates picked the 'right' answer. The questions themselves may be **flawed** and simplistic, however, so this may not reflect anything of actual value, such as a student's knowledge, understanding, skill or perception.

 4   **a** Give synonyms for the ten words in bold in Text 6B.

virtually	resolutely	lenient	stifle	scoff
tellingly	unwary	coached	fundamentally	flawed

b Use the three phrases below (in italics in the passage) in sentences of your own.
  i swear by   **ii** foster the fallacy   **iii** give the illusion of

c Look at the use of 'former' and 'latter' in the quotation from the passage below.

  '... differing opinions amongst supporters and critics; the *former* swear by them, while the *latter* are resolutely opposed.'
  i Write an explanation of how this pair of words is used, in this case and generally.
  ii Write a sentence of your own using this pair of words.

 5   **a** Select the true statements about multiple-choice tests, according to the passage, and discuss why it was difficult to make your choices.
  i   they are favoured by academic establishments
  ii they prove nothing
  iii they are easy
  iv they are controversial
  v   they contain simple questions

b Set your own question with a set of five multiple-choice answers based on the passage, and swap with a partner to answer each other's question. How difficult was it to get the right answer?

c After reading the passage and doing Activities 5a and 5b, are you in favour of multiple-choice testing or not? Say which piece of information in the passage persuaded you. Was it a fact or an opinion?

 6   **a** Read the key point on the next page to help you, and discuss in class:
  i   the definition of a fact and an opinion, and the differences between them
  ii how it is possible to distinguish between facts and opinions
  iii their purpose in discursive and argumentative writing or speaking.

Key point

Fact versus opinion

Many discursive and argumentative texts contain a mixture of facts (things that can be proved and are not disputed) and opinions, which are the views of the writer or someone being quoted in the text. One way of distinguishing them is to look at the verb accompanying them: a fact is likely to be introduced by the verb *to be*, e.g. 'It is the case that ...'; an opinion is likely to be introduced by a verb such as *claims*, *states*, or even just *says*. This warns the reader that the content has not been verified, and the information will probably contain the modal verbs *can*, *may* or *might*. However, you need to be careful when reading advertising or propaganda, which is deliberately biased and tries to convince you that the writer's belief is accepted fact.

b Identify the facts and opinions in Text 6B, and list them in two columns.

c Contribute to the columns collected on the board and see if others agree with you.

 Texts 6C and 6D on pages 80 and 81 are from Act I of Shakespeare's play *Macbeth*. In the speech in Text 6C, Macbeth gives reasons why he should not murder Duncan in order to become king of Scotland himself (as prophesied by the three witches he has met earlier in the day). King Duncan is coming to stay at his castle this evening.

7 Work with a partner, after listening to the speech read aloud.

a Write a paraphrase of the speech in modern English.

b List the five reasons Macbeth gives for deciding not to carry out the murder.

c Note down the different images you can identify.

d How would you describe Macbeth's state of mind, judging from his language?

e This speech is called a soliloquy. What do you think this might mean, and why is this theatrical device being used here? *– see Tip p90*

Text 6C

Macbeth chooses No

MACBETH
                           He's here in double trust:
First, as I am his kinsman and his subject,
Strong both against the deed; then, as his host,
Who should against his murderer shut the door,
Not bear the knife myself. Besides, this Duncan
Hath borne his faculties so meek, hath been
So clear in his great office, that his virtues
Will plead like angels, trumpet-tongued against
The deep damnation of his taking-off.
And pity, like a naked newborn babe
Striding the blast, or heaven's cherubim horsed
Upon the sightless couriers of the air,
Shall blow the horrid deed in every eye,
That tears shall drown the wind. I have no spur
To prick the sides of my intent, but only
Vaulting ambition, which o'erleaps itself
And falls on the other.

Tip

For Activity 7
Soliloquy

Meaning 'talking to oneself', a soliloquy is an old-fashioned dramatical device – much favoured by Shakespeare – to allow characters to communicate a thought process or how they are feeling to the audience, by thinking out loud. Sometimes there are other characters on stage at the time, but it is understood that they cannot hear what is being said in the soliloquy. The device is often used by the main characters in a tragedy to weigh up pros and cons for a course of action, as a kind of argument with themselves.

In Text 6D, Macbeth's wife comes to speak to him, and when he tells her he has decided against the murder, she tries to change his mind.

Lady Macbeth chooses Yes

MACBETH   We will proceed no further in this business:
                 He hath honoured me of late, and I have bought
                 Golden opinions from all sorts of people,
                 Which would be worn now in their newest gloss,
                 Not cast aside so soon.

LADY MACBETH   Was the hope drunk
                 Wherein you dressed yourself? Hath it slept since?
                 And wakes it now, to look so green and pale
                 At what it did so freely? From this time,
                 Such I account thy love. Art thou afeard
                 To be the same in thine own act and valour
                 As thou art in desire? Wouldst thou have that
                 Which thou esteem'st the ornament of life,
                 And live a coward in thine own esteem,
                 Letting 'I dare not' wait upon 'I would,'
                 Like the poor cat i' th'adage?

MACBETH   Prithee, peace.
                 I dare do all that may become a man;
                 Who dares do more is none.

LADY MACBETH   What beast was't, then,
                 That made you break this enterprise to me?
                 When you durst do it, then you were a man.
                 And, to be more than what you were, you would
                 Be so much more the man.

8 Work with a partner, after listening to the dialogue
read aloud.

a What are the two further reasons Macbeth gives in
   Text 6D for not proceeding with 'this business'?

b Summarise Lady Macbeth's argument in your
   own words.

c What language devices and persuasive techniques
   does she use?

9 Discuss the following questions with a partner, and tell the class your views.

a How would you describe the relationship between Macbeth and Lady Macbeth in Text 6D, giving textual evidence?

b What makes this dialogue so dramatic and engaging for an audience?

c Who do you think wins this argument, and why?

Text 6E

Choices

I thought I had a choice when I was young
and some young me decided what I did
and so became the me that now is sung,
the me from whom all other pasts are hid.

I think I have a choice this very day
and now will be deciding what I do
and so become the me that chose this way,
the me to whom some futures gave no clue.

I think I will have choices still to come
and me to be will claim decisions made
and so remain the me that hears the drum,
the me for whom there comes the last parade.

I hear no drummer but my own and so
no other times and pathways can I know.

Robert Stone

10 Work with a partner to comment on the following aspects of Text 6E. Copy and complete the table for class discussion.

	Comment
form	
rhyme scheme	A B A B
rhythm	10 syllables
language	
imagery	None

11 a Summarise in one sentence what the persona is arguing in Text 6E.

    b Compare this poem to Text 6A and list the similarities and
       differences in content and form.

    c Decide which of the two poems you prefer, and give reasons for
       your preference.

Read Text 6F and then work in a small group on Activities 12 and 13.

Text 6F

Mother Nature provides.
The earth gives birth to natural mineral water.
Water is the essence of life.

Silver Spring

is what it says on the label.
It comes sparkling and bubbling from a
mountain source.
It contains real minerals, for healthier bodies.
Its natural chemistry means a longer, better life.

Silver Spring

is the fresh taste of spring that puts a spring
in your step.
Get close to Mother Nature now.

12 a How does the advert try to make the reader believe that this is a
       necessary product?

    b List the words and phrases in the advert which are appealing, and
       explain their effect.

    c Discuss the name of the product and explain its connotations.

    d Summarise in one sentence of your own words what the advert is
       claiming.

    e Write a one-sentence profile of the consumer audience that the
       advert is aimed at.

13 **a** Make a copy of the table and write the associations of the word for each of these car model names.

Scirocco	
Golf	
Mondeo	
Ka	
Discovery	
Cherry	
Focus	
Silver Shadow	
Quattro	
Tigra	

b i Discuss and choose the five most appealing car model names.
ii Suggest three suitable car model names of your own.

c Write a half-page magazine advertisement for a product of your choice. Give it a name, a logo, and an image to accompany it. Use the tip below to help you.

For Activity 13c
Advertising structure and style

A print advertisement is a form of argumentative persuasive writing that makes an emotional appeal to the reader, to evoke the desire to own something, enjoy something, or to do the right thing. It will present only the positive side of what is on offer.

- *Structure:* Advertisements usually begin with an attention-catching device, such as an imperative, question, exclamation or categorical statement. This is then followed by evidence or details to support the initial claim. The ending is an implied warning that there is no time to lose in choosing and buying the product, and is often in the form of an imperative.
- *Style:* Advertisements use a lot of adjectives, often in the comparative or superlative form (though without stating what is being compared). They address the reader as 'You' and/or 'We' to represent people in general, implying that everyone has the same needs. The sentences are usually short, to give them clarity of meaning and instant impact. The language

may include clichés and other snappy, memorable phrases which rely on alliteration or puns. Foreign or exotic words may be used to make the product sound grander. The name of the product is likely to be insistently repeated. Lists give an impression of an abundance of qualities of the product and pleasures for the purchaser. The present tense is used (rather than the future, which takes more words and is less direct) to imply the reader is losing out on something they could already be benefiting from.

d Present your product idea to the class, with all members of your group making a contribution.
  i Explain the target market for it.
  ii Read out the advert in an appropriate tone of voice.
  iii Explain the connotations of your choice of name.
  iv Draw the logo on the board and explain its intended effect.
  v Describe and support your choice of image.

e The class will vote on the most persuasive advert and give reasons for their choice.

Text 6G

The Three Princes

Long ago on the Arabian Peninsula, when cities flourished along the major trade routes that stretched across the desert to transport spices, almonds and dates, there ruled in one of those cities a king whose daughter had come of marriageable age.

Three princes of nearby cities came to court her. But the princess   5
looked at them with alarm. One prince was bossy, the second prince was unclean in his habits, and the third suitor was vain.

'Father, I beg you, don't make me marry any of them!' she cried.

The king loved his daughter, but he didn't want to offend her suitors and risk angering his neighbouring city-states.   10

'I'll think about it,' he said. 'Come back tomorrow.'

The next day, he summoned the three suitors and the princess to his throne room.

'Each of you is a perfectly worthy suitor for my daughter's hand,' he said. 'Therefore, to make the correct decision I have determined   15
that the three of you must venture into the world for one year and

a day. Whoever returns with the most wondrous item will win my daughter's hand in marriage.'

The three princes set out together. After travelling for one week they came to a well that was located before a fork in the road, beyond which the road branched into three separate paths.   20

'Obviously, this is where we should part,' stated the first prince.

'Don't you think we know that?' said the second prince, wiping his dirty hands on his cloak.

'Listen carefully,' the first prince continued. 'One week before we   25
return to the palace, let's all meet at this well to compare what we found.'

'I only hope the maidens don't slow me down by falling in love with me,' said the third prince, throwing back his hair. 'It's such a nuisance.'

And so the three princes went their separate ways. When the time came to return to the well, each one followed his separate path   30
that led back to the well.

'You look a little the worse for wear,' said the first prince to the second. 'I'm fine,' said the second prince, blowing his nose onto his sleeve. 'What did you find?'

'Only a crystal ball,' said the first prince, as nonchalantly as   35
he could, 'that shows anything you want to see that's happening anywhere in the world.'

The other two were impressed (and a bit worried). Said the first prince to the second, 'What wondrous item did you find?'

From under his cloak the second prince unrolled a carpet. 'A   40
flying carpet. People who sit on it can be transported anywhere in the world they wish to go in minutes.'

'If they don't mind sitting next to you,' another prince murmured, holding his nose. And now it was the third prince's turn to show what he had brought.   45

'This vial,' said the third prince, 'holds a magical healing ointment. One dab of it will restore the health of anyone, no matter how sick. And they say if it's rubbed with true love, it can even restore youth.'

'Speaking of health,' said the second prince to the first, 'since you have a crystal ball, let's take a look at our princess and see how   50
she fares.'

The first prince waved his hands over the crystal ball; its cloudiness disappeared and was replaced with an image of the princess lying in her bed, still as death. Her father and the court physicians hovered over her. 'Isn't there anything you can do?'   55
said the king. 'Sire, we have done everything,' said the head court physician. 'I'm sorry, but she has very little time left.'

The three princes leapt up, alarmed. 'Alas!' cried the third prince. 'My ointment would heal her, but we're too far from the palace – we'll never get there in time!'   60

'Quick, everyone on my magic carpet,' said the second prince. 'We'll get there in a flash!'

Indeed, moments later the three princes were standing in the very room they had viewed through the crystal ball only minutes before. Everyone was so distraught they didn't notice the three princes had suddenly appeared in the room. Without a word, the third prince stepped up to the princess's bed and with his finger touched a dab of ointment on her forehead and set the ointment by her bedstand. She blinked and seconds later opened her eyes. Then she moved her head, and sat up. 'I feel better,' she said.

'It's a miracle!' cried the father, and he embraced his daughter.

Later that night, the three princes appeared before the king. 'Your majesty,' said the first prince, 'each of us may have located a magical item. But there is no doubt that my crystal ball is the most wondrous item of all. Without it, none of us would have known the princess was sick in the first place. I submit that mine is the most wondrous item and therefore I deserve the hand of the princess.'

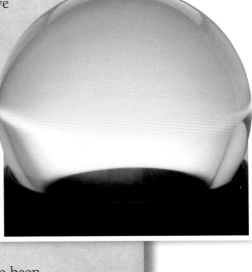

'With all due respect,' said the second prince, stepping forward, 'while it was informative to learn that the princess was sick, had we not been able to travel a week's journey in a blink of an eye on my flying carpet, that knowledge would have done us no good. I submit that mine is the most wondrous item and therefore I deserve the hand of the princess.'

'Good sire,' said the third prince. 'While it may have been useful to learn the princess was sick and was helpful to arrive here as quickly as we did, had we not had my magical ointment, all that knowledge and all that quickness would have been in vain. I submit that mine is the most wondrous item and therefore I deserve the hand of the princess.'

The king was perplexed. Each of the princes made a good argument. And since the question was so close, no matter which prince he selected, he was sure to raise the ire of the other two and their neighbouring city-states.

'I'll think about it,' he said. 'Come back tomorrow.'

That night, the king summoned his viziers to ask their advice. 'Sire,' said his head vizier, 'there is a wise old man who lives amongst us who hails from very far away, a distant country called Russia. He is well known for his sage advice, and if we allow him to make the decision, the communities of the princes who aren't chosen will get angry at a country far away, and not at us.'

65

70

90

95

100

'Excellent thought,' said the king. 'Summon him to court 105
tomorrow.'

The next day when the three princes arrived to hear which of
them would be selected, at court stood a very old man. He hobbled
on his cane and spoke in a whisper. The three princes repeated why
they thought they deserved the hand of the princess. 110

'As far as I'm concerned,' asserted the king, 'each of these fine
young men has an equal claim to my daughter's hand. And so,' he
turned to his guest, 'I am interested. You come from a faraway land.
What is your opinion?'

The old man coughed and cleared his throat. 'Your Majesty, first 115
allow me to say that it is an honour to be in your court.' He raised
a shaky hand toward the princes. 'There's no doubt that each of you
brought a wondrous item that saved the life of the princess. But in
my country, when it comes to marriage, there are those who say
that the young woman, whose happiness is at stake, should have 120
a say in the matter. And so I would ask our royal highness.' He
turned to her. 'Princess, whom do you wish to marry?'

Retold by Elaine L. Lindy

14 a Text 6G is a Saudi Arabian fairy tale. The ending of the story is
missing. Choose how you think it should end, adding another two
paragraphs to say:
  i who the princess chooses and why, in direct speech
  ii what the reactions to and consequences of her choice were.

b Read your ending to the class, which will vote on the best.

c Research the actual ending to the story to see how it compares with
your ending, and say which you prefer.

15 You are going to write a short story of your own which concerns
someone having to make an important choice. To write your story
you need to make choices about:

a the kind of choice that has to be made in the story, and the conflict
and tension caused by it

b the narrative viewpoint and voice

c the characters, their roles and relationships

d a setting for your story, in a time and a place, with descriptive detail

e an engaging opening, a climax, and an effective ending, whether
open or resolved.

UNIT 7 Education matters

This unit focuses on forming a view and practising persuasive techniques, looking at a range of non-fiction articles, a satirical poem and a drama extract. You will transform information to argument, design a poster and a publicity flyer, present a dialogue, as well as report on a survey and refute an argument.

Activities

1

a   What do you think about the education you have had so far?

b   What other types of education have you heard about, in different countries or in your own country?

c   If you were Minister for Education, what changes or improvements would you want to make to your country's education system?

Too many toys

Workaholic parents think they can **compensate** for the time they don't spend with their children by buying them more toys. But recent research suggests that this **ploy** is actually leading to children losing the ability to play properly. Younger children, in particular those aged five or under, can be overwhelmed by too much choice, and end up playing less than children with fewer, more valued toys and games. In addition, a **surfeit** of toys can prevent the development of other skills; parental time spent with the child, playing with them, reading or even singing to them, is developmentally far superior, regardless of parental income level.

This is the view of a professor of educational psychology, following a study of 3,000 children from the ages of three to five. She said that, 'When children own a large number of toys they are **distracted** and they do not learn or play well. They move from one to the other and do not settle to anything.'

Western parents now spend 5 billion dollars buying 423 million toys each year, according to the latest figures, amounting to an average of $500 per child. Research suggests that there are 8 billion dollars' worth of unused toys in homes in just one European country.

But there are signs of change. Some parents have begun to encourage their children to play outside, and to give them board games instead of guns and dolls. They even give them empty cardboard boxes: many toys restrict children's imaginations, whereas an empty box could become anything.

A professor of early childhood education at an American university thinks that parents should restrict their children's access to toys. He said: 'It is a myth that the children with the most toys are happier and cleverer than those who only have a few favourites, and whose parents don't rush out to buy the latest plaything.' The view of the experts is that having many toys creates a feeling of being

overwhelmed, and that the **fallacy** that more is better needs to be **eradicated** from the thinking of the professional classes in the west. Research has shown that having fewer toys leads to an increase in sharing toys with others, and to **communal** rather than isolated play, which can only be **beneficial** to child development.

2 a Give synonym words or phrases for the ten words in bold in Text 7A.

workaholic	compensate	ploy	surfeit	distracted
overwhelmed	fallacy	eradicated	communal	beneficial

b Say whether the following five statements are true, false or uncertain, according to the passage.
  i Children between three and five have more toys than other age groups.
  ii Children from poorer backgrounds develop better than those from affluent ones.
  iii A cardboard box is a better toy than a doll or a gun.
  iv Children brought up in western homes are likely to have too many toys.
  v The more toys children have, the more likely they are to be willing to share them.

c Summarise the argument of the passage in one sentence.

Text 7B is a blog. Some words have been removed.

Text 7B

Just Google it!

I'm in the middle of a fight. My mother and I can't agree on who was the actor who played the detective in the film we saw last week. Was it _Bob_? 'Just Google it,' my sister intervenes. Yesterday, I couldn't remember what singer _Dodo_ looked like. 'Just Google it,' my colleague told me. When I'd lost the recipe for my favourite _food_, my friend's answer was instant: 'Just Google it.'

Two words. It's become as simple as that to find the answer to most of life's questions. Hit Google and you'll know the answer to everything under the sun – and instantly. You could find out, for example, whether there is _care_, or why the _sun is rayno_, or even when _It's the 3rd_. You don't need to go to a shrink any more; the search engine can provide you with the sanest and best advice anyone has ever given. In fact there's even a Church of Google that believes that Google is all-knowing and therefore divine! But the god to whom we address all questions has taken the fun out of a fight. There is no scope for speculation any more – Google has ruined all my chances of being right on a bluff.

Google has been around for little more than a decade, but it has changed the way we remember for ever. It has tamed my enthusiasm to memorise things, but it has given me access to facts about the things I love. I don't think my father, at the age of 29, could have rattled off answers about who _robby_ was or what a _dodo_ is or when to _punch someone_ one after the other. Human help used to be needed to tell us how to prune a bonsai or to cook a _chick_ or to _punch_ a _dodo_.

The truth is, I am miserable and can't live without my search engine, either at work or at home. Google has helped me grow mentally – even though I am much less fit physically – when I happily sit at a desk the whole day long, just Googling.

Ruchira Hoon, _Hindustan Times_

3 For Activities 3 and 4 you are going to work with a partner on a copy of Text 7B.

   a Fill in the 12 spaces with examples of your own.

   b **i** Circle the use of triple structures.
      ii Underline the use of contrast/antithesis.
      iii Box the examples of informal, conversational language.

   c Comment in the margin on the effect of:
      i the title
      ii the opening sentence
      iii the final phrase of the passage, 'just Googling'.

4 **a** List the five positive aspects and the five negative aspects of Googling, according to Text 7B, in two columns.

   b Evaluate the points and come to a decision about which case is stronger, and why.

   c Analyse the structure of the article and make notes to explain why one side is stronger than the other, despite their having the same number of points.

For Activity 4c
Argumentative structure and support

In Text 7B there are the same number of points for and against Google, but the article gives more weight to the 'fors' by positioning the negative points early on and giving lots of examples for the positive points. To reverse the effect you would need to add examples to the negative side, as well as change the order of the material, so that most of the negative points are left to the end and the article starts with the positive material. The reader remembers the last thing they read, and this directs them to adopt that view on the issue.

Notice that the fact there is at least some attempt to present the opposite view in the text makes the reader more disposed to accept the writer's personal opinion; if no mention had been made of an alternative attitude or of any negative ideas, the reader might have decided that the text was unreflectingly biased, keeping something back in order to manipulate the audience, or serving the purpose of an advertising promotion.

Caught in the net

Mumbai: Karan was 17 when he first played the popular online game Counterstrike. Soon, an entire evening was not enough and he started skipping classes, eventually bunking off school entirely.

'We got a call from the school saying he had not been attending for four months,' said his father.

Karan, which is a **pseudonym** because he did not want to be identified, suffers from what doctors call an 'Internet addiction disorder'. Last week, as the internet turned 40, the first **residential** treatment centre for online addicts opened in the US.

According to **psychiatrists**, excessive internet use becomes **pathological** if it interferes with a person's daily life and if he or she suffers from withdrawal symptoms when deprived of access for more than an hour.

Karan has been undergoing counselling. **Anecdotal** evidence suggests he's among a rising number of people caught in the internet's web.

'I have been counselling six to eight new cases of internet addiction every month this year,' said Mumbai-based psychiatrist Dr Seema Hingorrany, adding that her patients ranged from 10-year-olds to those in their 50s. Many of them tell her that they don't see that there is any problem with surfing and game playing, even though they do very little else.

Neha Bhayana, *Hindustan Times*

5   **a i** Give synonym words or phrases for the five bold words in Text 7C. Work out their meaning by studying the context and thinking of other similar words.

ii Give a word or phrase which is the same part of speech to replace the underlined words.

b Learn the spellings of the five underlined words in the passage. First identify and study the 'hot spots', then test yourself using LCWC (Look, Cover, Write, Check).

c The passage is a news article, and therefore a piece of informative writing. Rewrite it as a piece of argumentative writing, using the same material in a different sequence and style. Give it to your teacher. Read 1css English book 122-123

6 a In a small group, devise a list of five questions about how much time is spent on the internet compared to how much time is spent talking to people face-to-face or during other activities.

b Using your questionnaire, survey ten of your peers in another class and record their answers.

c Compile a short report which gives the findings and draws conclusions. Read it to the rest of the class and compare your findings with theirs.

So much more than words

Picking up a book is one of the cheapest entertainments around. The simple act of reading – what you are doing now – has been characterised as everything from a silent conversation and a tool for building a better life to a refuge from reality and a technique for time travel. A story has the power not only to place you in another life, but also to connect you to otherwise indifferent individuals. With enough books and enough people, you build a shared culture.

Imagine that you couldn't read. This is the case for 774 million adults around the world. Those are the unlucky masses who have never had the tools to build a better life, taken refuge from reality, or time-travelled. Even worse, 75 million children will soon join them as illiterate adults. In a childhood that is often characterised by days with little to eat, sick or elderly relatives to care for, or dirty, airless factories to work in, not being able to read is an added punishment. It denies them any form of escape.

Learning to read and write has the amazing capacity to change lives. An education can increase your income; an education can teach you about disease; an education can make a person more confident, more responsible, more able to contribute to the lives of others and to their country. This is where the power of reading truly lies. It is that subtle force that can move mountains, as well as minds.

My hope is that reading, without which education is impossible, will finally be universally recognised and valued for its ability to bring personal and social development to the global community.

Queen Rania of Jordan, *Sunday Times Magazine*

7 With a partner, select items of content, features of syntax (grammar) and choices of vocabulary in the first three paragraphs of Text 7D. Copy and complete the table below, making notes on why each feature is effective.

	Content	Syntax	Vocabulary
Paragraph one			
Paragraph two			
Paragraph three			

8 a Write a paraphrase of the final paragraph of Text 7D.

b Identify the points the writer is making and combine them, in one paragraph of your own words, to give a summary of Queen Rania's argument.

c Discuss in class your own reading habits, making it clear whether or not you agree with Queen Rania's views, giving reasons.

9 Working in a group, you are going to make a poster to promote reading.

a First discuss how to promote reading for pleasure in your school. What are the 'resistance points'? See the tip below to help you.

For Activity 9a
Overcoming resistance

In order to be effective when writing or speaking persuasively, you have first to identify the likely reasons that the reader or listener would disagree with you, or with what you are trying to sell or promote. For instance, it may be the expense, or the novelty of the idea, or the possible danger involved. It is important to target these fears and include reassurance about them, such as stressing the low cost or the popularity or the safety of the product, in order to win over the audience.

b Decide on a slogan for a poster. This should be short and dramatic, using a language device such as alliteration, assonance or a pun to make it memorable.

c Design the poster, on a computer or by hand, considering layout, letter-style variations, colour and images. Display it in the school corridor or outside the library.

Text 7E

Touchy-feely robot to teach in school

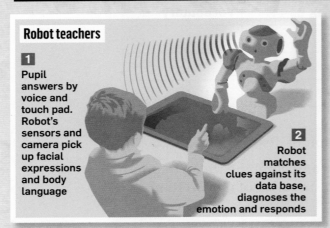

Robot teachers

1 Pupil answers by voice and touch pad. Robot's sensors and camera pick up facial expressions and body language

2 Robot matches clues against its data base, diagnoses the emotion and responds

Scientists are trying to create the world's first robot teacher with the capacity to respond to a child's moods and emotions in the classroom.

The personal, empathetic and human qualities that make a good teacher would first be analysed before being programmed into the robot.

Working one-to-one with the machine, children would be able to communicate through a touchscreen on their desks, the designers say.

The robot would gather information via sensors and cameras, allowing it to recognise emotions using clues such as the child's facial expressions and body language, to cross-reference against its database.

Although the project is intended to find new ways of teaching and learning – and will begin by training the robot to teach geography to pupils aged between 11 and 13 – the implications of endowing machines with the ability to recognise and respond to emotions are far wider. The unconventional teacher will be able to sense when one of its pupils is upset or struggling to cope. It would then provide the appropriate comfort and support.

If all goes to plan, the robot will be able to speak and move its head and arms, assess how well each child is doing and adapt its teaching style or material appropriately, just as its human equivalent should.

Some teachers have reacted with scepticism to this project, which is called Emote, saying that a large part of what makes a teacher effective is the building up of trust. Children are naturally curious and it is through conversations with their teachers that cognitive and emotional skills develop. A robot cannot know a child in the same way as a parent or teacher. Others say that we should not be scared of using new technologies to widen professional expertise in order to enhance teaching methods and improve the life chances of young people.

Liz Lightfoot, *Sunday Times*

10 **a** Which ten words in Text 7E mean the following (note that they do not occur in the order below):

providing	disbelief	ability	counterpart	sensitive to others' feelings
rational	compare	unorthodox	augment	instructed

b Copy the phrases below in your notebook and complete them by
supplying the correct preposition, without looking back at the
passage until you are ready to check your answers.
  i being programmed _____ the robot
  ii communicate _____ a touchscreen
  iii gather information _____ sensors
  iv the implications _____ endowing
  v respond _____ emotions

c i Write in one sentence of your own words an explanation of why
     some teachers object to robots being used as teachers.
  ii Write in one sentence of your own words an explanation of why
     some teachers think that it could be an advantage to use robots
     as teachers.
  iii Write a one-paragraph summary, in your own words, of the
     qualities of a good teacher. Read it to the class.

Text 7F

Head of English

Today we have a poet in the class.
A real live poet with a published book.
Notice the inkstained fingers girls. Perhaps
we're going to witness verse hot from the press.
Who knows. Please show your appreciation
by clapping. Not too loud. Now

sit up straight and listen. Remember
the lesson on assonance, for not all poems,
sadly, rhyme these days. Still. Never mind.
Whispering's, as always, out of bounds –
but do feel free to raise some questions.
After all, we're paying forty pounds.

Those of you with English Second Language,
see me after break. We're fortunate
to have this person in our midst.
Season of mists and so on and so forth.
I've written quite a bit of poetry myself,
am doing Kipling with the Lower Fourth.

Right. That's enough from me. On with the Muse.
Open a window at the back. We don't
want winds of change about the place.
Take notes, but don't write reams. Just an essay

> on the poet's themes. Fine. Off we go.
> Convince us that there's something we don't know.
>
> Well. Really. Run along now girls. I'm sure
> that gave an insight to an outside view.
> Applause will do. Thank you
> very much for coming here today. Lunch
> in the hall? Do hang about. Unfortunately
> I have to dash. Tracey will show you out.
>
> Carol Ann Duffy

11 In groups discuss Text 7F and make notes under the following headings. Your teacher will assess your participation in the discussion.

a Who is talking to whom in the poem, and where, and why?

b How would you describe the personality and attitudes of the English teacher? What is the evidence?

c How do we know that the teacher does not approve of the visiting poet? Find as much support as you can.

d The aim of this poem is satirical (mocking and criticising). Who and what is being satirised, and why?

e Define this kind of poem. What effects are possible when using this form?

Key point

Dramatic monologue

A poem in which a single speaker who is not the poet talks, as in a play, to an internal silent audience, and sometimes also performs actions, is called a dramatic monologue. This form is traditional in satirical verse as it allows the speaker to reveal and condemn themselves out of their own mouth. Readers can infer what is unacceptable about the personality and beliefs of the speaker without the need for the poet to say anything. It also allows irony and sometimes humour to be present, as the speaker does not of course realise what they are giving away and what a fool they are making of themselves.

   This form also has the effect of making the speaker seem dominant over the other people who are present but not given any words to speak. The speaker is thus conveyed as being overbearing, or impolite, or as thinking themselves superior to everyone else, and this adds to the satire.

12 With a partner, you are going to write and perform a dialogue based on Text 7F.

a We can infer what the poet would think and feel about the way the Head of English is behaving and speaking in Text 7F. Make some notes about her views on the teacher, on the teaching of poetry, and on the way she was treated during the visit.

b Plan, write and improve an argument dialogue between the poet and the teacher, beginning with the poet saying, as she is leaving: 'I won't be staying for lunch after all.'
Give about 10 short speeches to each speaker. They should be firmly critical, but not abusive.

c Perform your dialogue in role to the class. Discuss and evaluate your own performance and that of the others.

In this drama extract a barrister cross-examines a mother who is being prosecuted for failure to provide adequate education for her two children.

Text 7G

HEALEY:	Is there any difference then, so far as you are concerned, between life for your children and education?
SALLY WYATT:	No, life is education. All life. For most people, education has become a preparation for work, then life becomes work. We do not believe that is education.
HEALEY:	As far as you are concerned, every experience they have from the moment they wake up until they go to sleep is part of their education.
SALLY WYATT:	There are no set hours, if that's what you mean. Yes, it's a continuous education. It isn't a matter of what facts you know – more a matter of finding and getting the facts you need, learning how to use what you've got in a constantly changing situation. That's not pie in the sky, that's a tough assignment. Children with heads stuffed full of facts and figures do not interest me. The quest for ideas, that is what we are trying to achieve.
HEALEY:	If, for example, Michael wrote a story or a letter – if he could write – would you correct it?
SALLY WYATT:	If he asked me to correct it, yes.

HEALEY:	If not, you would leave it uncorrected.
SALLY WYATT:	Yes.
HEALEY:	You would allow him to send the letter uncorrected.
SALLY WYATT:	Yes, of course. What is important is the child's sense of achievement, not the quality of the spelling or punctuation.
HEALEY:	And yet Michael is eleven and still cannot read, and Laura did not learn to read until she was sixteen.
SALLY WYATT:	That is correct.
HEALEY:	Do you not think she might have learned to read much earlier if she had gone to school in the usual way?
SALLY WYATT:	That's not important. You keep looking for a standard. You must be here at such and such a time. That's what happens in schools. It's a fiercely competitive attitude and it sets people against each other right from the start.
HEALEY:	Yes, but what you are describing to me as an alternative, Mrs Wyatt, is nothing more than a creative form of truancy. By adopting your policy of 'the children will learn when they want to learn to read', you are neglecting – more than that – you are abandoning the learning potential of your children to read or write. You have made no active attempts to rectify Michael's basic lack of skill in this area. By denying him the facilities of a full-time education, as the law requires, you are failing to cause your son to receive education 'suitable to his age, ability and aptitude'. How can this kind of negligence be categorized as efficient education?

David Leland, *Flying Into the Wind*

13 Work with a partner.

a Select some phrases for both speakers to show how they use language differently.

b Look at the questions asked by Mr Healey. What do you notice about them?

c Explain how courtroom dramas create tension and suspense by their generic format, referring to the extract. Read the tip on the next page to help you.

For Activity 13c
Courtroom drama

Trials are adversarial, i.e. there are opposing sides, and the battle comes to a climax when a defence witness is being cross-examined by lawyers for the prosecution, or vice versa. The tension is built up through short exchanges, one-liners, and we wait to see who will make a mistake and give something away, or say something which shocks the jury. Both speakers must choose their words very carefully, as they are being recorded and a single wrong word can change the outcome. The audience becomes engaged enough to take sides, according to which character they empathise with, and hope for a verdict of guilty or innocent, so that suspense is built up.

14 a Discuss and decide which side you think the audience is meant to take in Text 7G.

b Copy out the phrases and sentences which influenced your decision.

c Explain exactly how the language persuades the audience to adopt that viewpoint.

15 Work with a partner.

a Write a rebuttal of Sally Wyatt's standpoint, using ideas of your own as well as those in the passage.

Key point

Producing a rebuttal

A rebuttal is the refutation or contradiction of someone's views. Court cases and debates rely on rebuttal, whereby one's own position is strengthened by being able to expose the alternative view as unfounded and unworthy of being believed. Each claim or opinion should be taken in turn and discredited using opposing arguments and counter-evidence, which simultaneously builds up one's own standpoint.

b Write a dialogue in the style of a courtroom exchange between a prosecuting barrister and a defendant. Write about a page of short question-and-answer speeches.

c Perform your dialogue to the class, which will judge which character wins the argument.

16 Work in small groups on a publicity flyer for your school.

a Collect points you would make about your own school if you were asked to recommend it. Think about many different aspects of the school, e.g. curriculum, academic results, facilities and equipment, sporting opportunities and achievements, extra-curricular clubs and trips, teachers' qualifications.

b Think about the audience the flyer is intended for, and what they will want to know about the school, e.g. where it is and how easy it is to get to, whether there are scholarships or an entrance test.

c Decide how to organise the layout of an A4 flyer to promote the school in the local area. Think about headings.

d Think about vocabulary, tone and sentence types to suit the purpose of persuasion. How formal should it be?

e Write the flyer as a group task, each contributing to the way it is written. Give it to your teacher to display in the classroom.

UNIT 8 Caring and sharing

This unit focuses on the language of persuasion and pathos. You will respond to a news story and a fiction story, a diary entry, an appeal letter, and informative articles. You will look at more punctuation, vocabulary and grammar structures. Tasks include designing a poster, creating dialogue, collating material in texts, and writing a charity appeal letter.

Activities

1 Make notes on the following in preparation for a class discussion.

a What do you think one should care about most: oneself, one's family, one's community, one's country, or the planet?

b Which charities do you support or would you consider supporting, and why?

c If you won or inherited a vast amount of money, how would you spend it?

Ten facts about malaria

- a preventable disease that affects almost half the world's population and causes over 660,000 deaths per year
- an infection caused by the malaria parasite entering the bloodstream, usually through the bite of an infected mosquito
- over 90 percent of deaths occur in sub-Saharan Africa
- 3,000 children die of malaria every day
- only the female mosquito transmits the disease
- sleeping under a mosquito net is essential in affected regions
- children under five are most at risk
- the disease exists in 109 countries in the world
- mosquitoes breed where there is an abundance of humidity and rain
- symptoms are fever, chills and headache

2 Work in a small group to plan a web campaign to raise awareness of the problem of malaria.

a Decide on a slogan/website name for your campaign.

b Design a web poster and select some of the facts in Text 8A to use in it.

c Write a statement about malaria as a header for the website, to explain why it is such a serious disease.

d Decide on an image to illustrate the home page.

e Swap posters with other groups and evaluate their effectiveness, writing your comments on a 'post-it'.

Text 8B

Shameful waste

When I was at school, we had to eat everything on our plates, no matter how nasty, because starving children in Africa would have been grateful for it – something incomprehensible to schoolchildren today. But the world is smaller now, and there is an obvious relationship between what I eat and what others don't, and can't. Increasingly, people understand that wastefulness affects everybody across the globe: it squanders the world's plenty and leaves pollution, overcrowding, disease and famine in its wake.

Somehow that doesn't stop us wasting food in astonishing quantities. As much as half of all the food produced in the world – 2 billion tonnes – ends up as waste. It never makes it to the plate. This is enough to startle anyone out of statistics fatigue.

The explanation is twofold. In the developing world poor farming practices, muddled. Every time my eyes dropped closed I thought I was walking, the grass was long, I saw the elephants, I didn't know we were away.

But our grandmother was still strong, she could still stand up, she knows how to write and she signed for us. Once every month the food truck comes to the clinic. Our grandmother takes along one of the cards she signed and when it has been punched we get a sack of mealie-meal. There are wheelbarrows to take it back to the tent. On another day, every month, the church leaves a pile of old clothes in the clinic yard. Our grandmother has another card to get punched, and then we can choose something: I have two dresses, two pants and a jersey, so I can go to school. Our grandmother hasn't been able to buy herself a pair of shoes for church yet, but she has bought black school shoes and polish to clean them with for my first-born brother and me. Every morning, my first-born brother and I clean our shoes. Our grandmother makes us sit on our mat with our legs straight out so she can look carefully at our shoes to make sure we have done it properly. No other children in the tent have real school shoes. When we three look at them it's as if we are in a real house again, with no war, no away.

Nadine Gordimer, *The Ultimate Safari*

7 Work on a copy of Text 8D.

a Some of the commas used in Text 8D to suggest a child's train of thought are at the end of a sentence. Decide which ones, and choose whether to replace them with a full stop or a semi-colon.

b There are places in the passage where a comma would normally be used but is missing. Insert commas, both necessary and optional, in the right places.

c What type of sentences are used in the passage? What is their effect?

8 **a** How many tenses are used in paragraph one of Text 8D? Name them and give one example of each.

b What is the effect of the narrator referring to her brothers not by their names but as 'first-born' and 'little brother'?

c In the passage is the sentence 'He likes just to lie about on our grandmother all day'. Copy and complete the table below for the verbs *to lie* and *to lay*.

present	past simple	past participle	present participle
lie	lay	lied	lieing
lay	lay	layed	laying

For Activity 8c
Lie and *lay*

Because the past tense of the verb *to lie* is the same as the present tense of the verb *to lay*, confusion often occurs between these two verbs.

'Lie' (not to be confused with telling lies) means to be in a horizontal position and is not followed by an object, e.g. 'I will lie on the floor'. It is often followed by a preposition such as 'on' or 'down'. It is an irregular verb.

'Lay' is followed by an object and means to place something, e.g. 'I will lay the cloth on the table'. It is a regular verb except for spelling of the past participle.

9 **a** Text 8D is fictional autobiography. Why do you think the writer chose this genre to highlight the difficulties of life as a refugee in South Africa rather than non-fiction?

b What makes the greatest impression on you in the passage about the life of a refugee?

c What are the most poignant phrases in the passage, the ones which make you feel sorry for the narrator? Discuss your choices in class and the reasons why you made them.

For Activity 9c
Evoking pathos

Some writing has the aim of making the reader feel pity for a character and the situation they find themselves in. This is known as pathos. Ways of evoking pathos are to mention physical suffering, such as lack of food or illness, and mental suffering, such as loneliness or fear. The younger the child and the older the adult, the more vulnerable they are and the more the reader feels sorry for them. The context of war and being a refugee is a situation which always demands a sympathetic response from the reader, because refugees are innocent victims and we would all hate to lose as much and to find ourselves in such a desperate situation.

10 **a** The account in Text 8D is written by an adult pretending to be a child. How are you able to tell this?

b Why do you think that the writer adopts the viewpoint and voice of a child?

c Rewrite paragraph four in an adult voice.

Text 8E is an extract from the diary of Anne Frank, a 14-year-old Jewish girl whose family and another family were in hiding in the Netherlands during its occupation in the Second World War. She calls her diary Kitty, and her father Pim. Margot is her elder sister. She has written a letter to her father complaining about his disapproval of her growing affection for Peter, the teenage boy in the other family, and insisting that she is now independent.

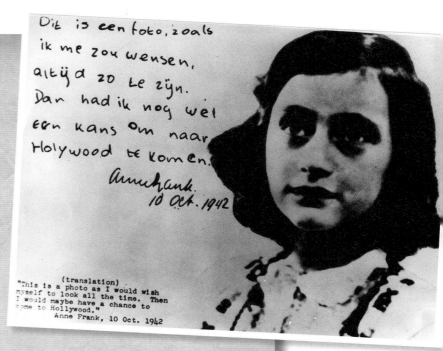

Dit is een foto, zoals ik me zou wensen, altijd zo te zijn. Dan had ik nog wel een kans om naar Holywood te komen.

Annefrank.
10 Oct. 1942

(translation)
"This is a photo as I would wish myself to look all the time. Then I would maybe have a chance to come to Hollywood."
Anne Frank, 10 Oct. 1942

Dearest Kitty,
Last night before dinner I tucked the letter I'd written into Father's pocket. According to Margot, he read it and was upset for the rest of the evening. (I was upstairs washing up!) Poor Pim, I might have known what the effect of such an epistle would be. He's so sensitive! I immediately told Peter not to ask questions or say anything more. Pim's said nothing else to me about the matter. Is he going to?

Yours, Anne M. Frank

Dearest Kitty,
Father and I had a long talk yesterday afternoon. I cried my eyes out, and he cried too. Do you know what he said to me, Kitty?

'I've received many letters in my lifetime, but none as hurtful as this. You, who have had so much love from your parents. You, whose parents have always been ready to help you, who have always defended you, no matter what. You talk of not having to account to us for your actions! You feel you've been wronged and left to your own devices. No, Anne, you've done us a great injustice… No, Anne, *we* have done nothing to deserve such a reproach!'

Oh, I've failed miserably. This is the worst thing I've ever done in my entire life. I used my tears to show off, to make myself seem important so he'd respect me. I've certainly had my share of unhappiness, and everything I said about Mother is true. But to accuse Pim, who's so good and who's done everything for me – no, that was too cruel for words.

It's good that someone has finally cut me down to size, has broken my pride, because I've been far too smug. Not everything Mistress Anne does is good! Anyone who deliberately causes such pain to someone they say they love is despicable, the lowest of the low!

What I'm most ashamed of is the way that Father has forgiven me; he said he's going to throw the letter in the stove, and he's being so nice to me now, as if *he* were the one who'd done something wrong. Well, Anne, you still have a lot to learn. It's time you made a beginning, instead of looking down on other people and always blaming them!

I've known a lot of sorrow, but who hasn't at my age? I've been putting on an act, but was hardly even aware of it. I've felt lonely, but never desperate! Not like Father, who once ran out into the street with a knife so that he could put an end to it all. I've never gone that far.

I should be deeply ashamed of myself, and I am. What's done can't be undone, but at least you can keep it from happening again. I'd like to start all over again, and that shouldn't be difficult, now that I have Peter. With him supporting me, I *know* I can do it! I'm not alone any more. I have my books, my writing and my diary. I'm not all that ugly, or that stupid, I have a sunny disposition, and I want to develop a good character!

Yes, Anne, you knew full well that your letter was unkind and untrue, but you were actually proud of it! I'll take Father as my example once again, and I *will* improve myself.

Yours, Anne M. Frank

Anne Frank, *The Diary of a Young Girl*

11 **a** Rephrase the following metaphors in Text 8E in your own words:

cut me down to size   putting on an act   sunny disposition

b Why are italicised words used in the passage?

c What is the effect of so many exclamations and questions in the passage?

12 a What is the effect of the large number of simple sentences in Text 8E?

b What is the effect of including a speech within the passage?

c Look at the punctuation of this sentence from the passage.

> *No, Anne, you've done us a great injustice.*

How would the meaning have been different if it had been written:

> *No Anne; you've done us a great injustice.*

Key point

Clarifying punctuation

Punctuation is a necessary device for preventing ambiguity, as well as for indicating the grammar, construction and intention of sentences. In Activity 12c the use of the commas shows who is being spoken to and that her name is not part of the meaning of the sentence. When necessary punctuation is left out, or wrong punctuation is used, unclear and possibly unfortunate utterances can be made, as in 'Let's eat grandma' as opposed to 'Let's eat, grandma.' It is not only commas one has to be careful not to leave out: 'A woman without her man is nothing' is very different from 'A woman: without her man is nothing', and there are many other examples of this kind.

13 a What is the effect in Text 8E of the writer:
   i addressing herself as Anne?
   ii calling the diary Kitty?
   iii signing the diary entries?

b What can you infer about the writer's feelings towards her mother? Support your answer with reference to the passage.

c Compare Texts 8D and 8E, both of which give a child's perspective of events and relationships.

Text 8F on the next page is a charity appeal letter to raise money and support for snow leopards threatened with extinction.

Text 8F

Dear Supporter

The solitary and elusive snow leopard has lived undisturbed in the mountains of central Asia for thousands of years. But poaching and pressures from unsustainable human development are now threatening the future of this stunning and unique creature. It is extremely vulnerable to the activities of people – and is now classed as endangered.

Populations of snow leopards are in decline throughout their natural habitat – with as few as 300 now thought to be left in the Himalayan kingdom of Nepal. Life is very hard for them in these rugged mountains, with declining food sources.

It is vital that we act now – or risk losing them in the wild for ever. Will you help us protect the last remaining snow leopards in the Himalayas?

A four-man patrol team monitors the population, checking known snow leopard areas to keep track of what is happening to them. The team advises locals on how to protect their livestock, so that the snow leopards are not shot in retaliation for attacking sheep and goats.

Money is needed urgently to enable this team to continue their essential work in saving the few remaining snow leopards.

By sending us a donation you will be helping us to protect the beautiful snow leopard.

Your generosity really could make a huge difference.

John Barker
Species programme manager
WWF

14 Work with a partner.

   a What is the structure, i.e. the order of the content, of Text 8F?

   b List the adjectives used in the letter to describe snow leopards. What can you say about them?

c Identify usages of the following in the letter, and explain their
   purpose:
   i   intensifiers
   ii time adverbials
   iii personal pronouns.

The future will have lost many species of animal. Tigers may be one of them.

Hunted for their pelt and bones and losing their habitat and prey, tiger populations are threatened throughout their natural habitats. In many places, they struggle for survival with **burgeoning** human populations competing for similar resources.

For over 1,000 years, tigers have been hunted as status symbols, for decorative items such as wall and floor coverings, as souvenirs and curios, and for use in traditional Asian medicines.

Hunting for sport probably caused the greatest decline in tiger populations up until the 1930s. In many areas tigers were also regarded as a pest that needed to be **exterminated**.

Between 1940 and the late 1980s, the greatest threat was loss of habitat due to human population expansion and activities such as logging. In the early 1990s, the trade in tiger bone for traditional medicines became a major threat.

Many countries lack the **capacity** and resources to properly monitor tiger and prey populations. Policies **conducive** to ensuring long-term survival of the tiger are often lacking. Where they do exist, **implementation** is often ineffective.

15 Work in pairs.

a Give synonyms for the five words in bold in Text 8G.

   burgeoning exterminated capacity conducive implementation

b Summarise the content of Text 8G in one complex sentence.

c i   What kind of writing is the passage and what is its purpose?
   ii How would you describe the style of the passage, and what is its effect?

Text 8H

Threats to tigers

Human activities are the principal cause of declining tiger numbers. Hunting was a major cause of **mortality** in the past, both for **trophies** and as part of organised pest control measures. Poaching and illegal killing, for example by livestock owners, remains one of today's major threats to the survival of this species, particularly with the growing demand for tiger bones in Oriental 'medicine'.

The demand for remedies made from tiger parts has grown due to increasing **affluence** in Asia, and laws preventing international trade in tiger parts are largely ignored. Hong Kong is the main importer of tiger products, with tiger bone the most used part. The bones are crushed to be used in anti-inflammatory drugs for rheumatism and arthritis, among many other uses. The trade in tiger skins is also increasing.

Habitat loss has occurred throughout much of the tiger's range and is now severely threatening its survival; as land becomes rapidly developed to meet the increasing demands of the Asian population, tiger populations become isolated in remaining **fragments** of wilderness and **ultimately** die out. The tiger's natural prey species have declined in numbers due to over-hunting, which has led tigers in some areas to turn to domestic livestock as a source of food, inevitably causing conflict with local farmers.

Conservation

Of the six surviving subspecies of tiger, the futures of the South China tiger and the Siberian tiger seem particularly **bleak**. Recent extensive surveys resulted in no sightings. India has the greatest number of tigers, but even the Bengal tiger population is estimated at no more than 2,500 individuals. The combined global figure for all remaining subspecies is estimated at between 3,200 and 4,000 tigers.

The Indian government established Project Tiger in 1973, with the aim of conserving the country's tiger population. Within India there are currently 21 tiger reserves, although these are increasingly threatened by human pressures on the land. The key to the survival of the tiger is the **maintenance** of large tracts of **adjacent** habitat, but protection of this species is complicated by its man-eater reputation and by the threat it poses to livestock. The involvement and commitment of local people will be vital for the future **sustainability** of this most **regal** of cats.

16 a Give synonyms for the following ten words as used in Text 8H in bold.

mortality   trophies   affluence   fragments   ultimately
bleak   maintenance adjacent   sustainability regal

b How does the style of writing of Text 8H differ from that of Text 8G?

c Which of the two texts did you find more persuasive of the need to act urgently to save the tiger, and why? Did everyone in the class agree?

17 You are going to write a charity appeal letter to raise money to help save tigers. You should explain the plight of the tiger and the measures needed to save it. Use the key point below to help you, and adopt the style of Text 8F.

a Select the information you will use from each of Texts 8G and 8H.

b Plan how to regroup and restructure the information, interweaving the facts and ideas from both of the passages, to give your letter a strong opening and ending, and to avoid repetition of the facts.

c Think about paragraphing and sentence length, and the choice of emotive and powerful vocabulary.

d Write a draft of the letter, of about one page, addressed 'Dear Supporter'.

e Rewrite the draft, making improvements and checking accuracy of expression. Give it to your teacher.

Key point

Making an appeal

For a piece of writing to be persuasive enough to make someone want to give money in support of a cause, it has to evoke guilt and pity: guilt that something terrible is happening and that the reader is doing nothing to help stop it; pity for the victim and a desire to relieve the situation.
This is a particular kind of persuasive writing:
- it differs from argument, which aims to make a convincing case but does not require anything from the reader other than their agreement
- it differs from informative writing, which does not try to evoke any emotion from the reader but has the aim of enlightening them
- it differs from discursive writing, which presents a range of opinions to entertain but does not ask the reader to adopt any of them.

UNIT 9 Crime and law

This unit includes a news article, a brochure and short stories, and practises the skills of predicting, continuing a narrative, inferring, comparing, hotseating, and identifying reader positioning and irony. You will design a poster and cartoon strip, and write a character sketch, a news report, a complaint letter and a short story.

Activities

1 **a** Discuss as a class how you feel about the laws in your country. Consider what is and isn't illegal, and the age at which the laws apply.

b Give examples of popular films and books that include a courtroom scene. Explain why you think readers and viewers enjoy these scenes.

c Detective fiction is one of the most popular kinds of novel. Give examples of the names of well-known detectives. Why do readers enjoy this kind of writing?

Text 9A is adapted from a pamphlet advising people how to prevent their possessions from being stolen.

A thief only needs a moment to make off with your valuables. Your coat hung up in a restaurant, your bag beside your chair, your mobile phone on the table while you pay the bill… all are **vulnerable** if you look away for a second. So try to be careful at all times. The same is true of your wallet or purse. Pickpockets often work in teams – while one **distracts** you, the other is picking your pocket. If someone bumps into you, check that you still have your money. Cafés, public transport and shopping areas are the places where most thefts occur.

Cash is a favourite target for thieves. So always try to avoid carrying large amounts of it. Always memorise your PIN number for your cash **dispensing** cards; do not carry it with you and never **disclose** it to anyone. Leaving cash on view anywhere is an open invitation. Someone could reach through a car window to take it, or steal it from your desk, or snatch it from your hand.

Bicycles are stolen by the millions every year. They are a popular target for thieves because they can easily be sold. Sometimes thieves collect a whole vanload of bicycles. They should be locked whenever they are left on the street, even if you are just popping into a shop very briefly. Mark the frame with your name or postcode. It will help the police return it to you if it is recovered – they have thousands of unclaimed, unidentifiable bicycles. The best kind of bicycle lock is made of a loop of solid metal. Chains **deter** casual thieves, but can be easily cut with the right equipment. Always lock your bicycle to something immovable, like a railing.

Eight out of ten burglaries occur when a house or flat is empty. So don't advertise your absence when you are on holiday or out shopping. Fit time switches to turn your house lights on after dark. Don't leave valuable items, such as DVDs and laptops, visible through the window. Doors need the strongest possible locks, and windows can also be made more secure with a lock requiring a key.

Adapted from *Practical Ways to Crack Crime*

2 a i Give synonyms for the five words in bold in Text 9A.

vulnerable   distracts   dispensing   disclose   deter

ii Change the words to their noun form.

b Give the part of speech for the following five words, as used in the first paragraph of the passage.

valuables   hung   second   picking   public

c Many of the sentences in the passage begin with 'So'. You have learned that *so* is a coordinating connective not normally used to begin sentences, so why do you think the writer does this?

3 Work in a small group on Text 9A to design a poster to remind people what they must do to protect their possessions.

a Identify the topic sentences and select other relevant material from the passage.

b Decide on the order in which to use the material, and ways to phrase it appropriately and concisely.

c Design the poster, including a heading slogan and an illustration (this may be done on a computer) and display it in the classroom.

Text 9B is the beginning of the first of a series of detective novels set in Botswana.

Mma Ramotswe had a detective agency in Africa, at the foot of Kgale Hill. These were its **assets**: a tiny white van, two desks, two chairs, a telephone, and an old typewriter. Then there was a teapot, in which Mma Ramotswe – the only lady private detective in Botswana – brewed redbush tea. And three mugs – one for herself, one for her   5
secretary, and one for the client. What else does a detective agency really need? Detective agencies rely on human **intuition** and intelligence, both of which Mma Ramotswe had in **abundance**. No **inventory** would ever include those, of course.

But there was also the view, which again could appear on   10
no inventory. How could any such list describe what one saw when one looked out from Mma Ramotswe's door? To the front, an acacia tree, the thorn tree which dots the wide edges of the Kalahari; the great white thorns, a warning; the olive-grey leaves, by contrast, so delicate. In its branches, in the late afternoon, or   15
in the cool of the early morning, one might see a Go-Away Bird, or hear it, rather. And beyond the acacia, over the dusty road, the roofs of the town under a cover of trees and scrub bush; on the horizon, in a blue **shimmer** of heat, the hills, like improbable, overgrown termite-mounds.   20

Everybody called her Mma Ramotswe, although if people had wanted to be formal, they would have addressed her as Mme Mma Ramotswe. This is the right thing for a person of **stature**, but which she had never used of herself. So it was always Mma Ramotswe, rather than Precious Ramotswe, a name which very   25
few people employed.

She was a good detective, and a good woman. A good woman in a good country, one might say. She loved her country, Botswana, which is a place of peace, and she loved Africa, for all its **trials**.

I am not ashamed to be called an African **patriot**, said Mma   30
Ramotswe. I love all the people whom God made, but I especially
know how to love the people who live in this place. They are my
people, my brothers and sisters. It is my duty to help them to
solve the mysteries in their lives. That is what I am called to do.

In idle moments, when there were no **pressing** matters to be   35
dealt with, and when everybody seemed to be sleepy from the
heat, she would sit under her acacia tree. It was a dusty place to
sit, and the chickens would occasionally come and peck about her
feet, but it was a place which seemed to encourage thought. It was
here that Mma Ramotswe would contemplate some of the issues   40
which, in everyday life, may so easily be pushed to one side.

Everything, thought Mma Ramotswe, has been something
before. Here I am, the only lady private detective in the whole of
Botswana, sitting in front of my detective agency. But only a few
years ago there was no detective agency, and before that, before   45
there were even any buildings here, there were just the acacia
trees, and the river-bed in the distance, and the Kalahari over
there, so close.

In those days there was no Botswana even, just the
Bechuanaland Protectorate, and before that again there was   50
Khama's Country, and lions with the dry wind in their manes.
But look at it now: a detective agency, right here in Gaborone,
with me, the fat lady detective, sitting outside and thinking these
thoughts about how what is one thing today becomes quite
another thing tomorrow.   55

Mma Ramotswe set up the No. 1 Ladies' Detective Agency with
the **proceeds** of the sale of her father's cattle. He had owned a
big herd, and had no other children; so every single beast, all one
hundred and eighty of them, including the white Brahmin bulls
whose grandparents he had bred himself, went to her. The cattle   60
were moved from the cattle post, back to Mochudi where they
waited, in the dust, under the eyes of the chattering herd boys,
until the livestock agent came.

They fetched a good price, as there had been heavy rains that
year, and the grass had been lush. Had it been the year before,   65
when most of that southern part of Africa had been *racked* by
drought, it would have been a different matter. People had *dithered*
then, wanting to hold on to their cattle, as without your cattle you
were naked; others, feeling more desperate, sold, because the rains
had failed year after year and they had seen the animals become   70
thinner and thinner. Mma Ramotswe was pleased that her father's
illness had prevented his making any decision, as now the price
had gone up and those who had held on were well rewarded.

'I want you to have your own business,' he said to her on his
death bed. 'You'll get a good price for the cattle now. Sell them
and buy a business. A butchery maybe. Whatever you like.' 75

She held her father's hand and looked into the eyes of the man
she loved beyond all others, her Daddy, her wise Daddy, whose
lungs had been filled with dust in those mines and who had
scrimped and saved to make life good for her. 80

It was difficult to talk through her tears, but she managed to
say: 'I'm going to set up a detective agency. Down in Gaborone. It
will be the best one in Botswana. The No. 1 Agency.'

For a moment her father's eyes opened wide and it seemed as if
he was struggling to speak. 85

'But ... but ...'

But he died before he could say anything more, and Mma
Ramotswe fell on his chest and wept for all the dignity, love and
suffering that died with him.

She had a sign painted in bright colours, which was then set up just 90
off the Lobatse Road, on the edge of town, pointing to the small
building she had purchased: THE NO. 1 LADIES' DETECTIVE
AGENCY. FOR ALL CONFIDENTIAL MATTERS AND ENQUIRIES.
SATISFACTION GUARANTEED FOR ALL PARTIES. UNDER
PERSONAL MANAGEMENT. 95

After a slow start, she was rather surprised to find that her
services were in considerable demand. She was consulted about
missing husbands, about the creditworthiness of potential
business partners, and about suspected fraud by employees. In
almost every case, she was able to come up with at least some 100

information for the client; when she could not, she *waived* her fee, which meant that virtually nobody who consulted her was dissatisfied. People in Botswana liked to talk, she discovered, and the mere mention of the fact that she was a private detective would let loose a positive outpouring of information on all   105
sorts of subjects. It *flattered* people, she concluded, to be approached by a private detective, and this effectively loosened their tongues.

Alexander McCall Smith, *The No. 1 Ladies' Detective Agency*

4 a Use the ten nouns in bold in Text 9B in a sentence each to show you understand their meaning as used in the passage:

assets	intuition	abundance	inventory	shimmer
stature	trials	patriot	pressing	proceeds

  b Give the meaning of the five verbs in italics in the passage:

racked   dithered   scrimped   waived   flattered

  c i Rephrase the following in positive form:

virtually nobody who consulted her was dissatisfied.

   ii What is the effect of the use of a double negative?

5 a Without looking at the passage until you have finished, copy and punctuate the following extract from Text 9B.

Mma Ramotswe had a detective agency in Africa at the foot of Kgale Hill these were its assets a tiny white van two desks two chairs a telephone and an old typewriter then there was a teapot in which Mma Ramotswe the only lady private detective in Botswana brewed redbush tea and three mugs one for herself one for her secretary and one for the client what else does a detective agency really need detective agencies rely on human intuition and intelligence both of which Mma Ramotswe had in abundance no inventory would ever include those of course.

  b There are parts of the passage which could have had inverted commas around them. Decide where they are and explain why they are needed.

  c Comment on the effect of the use of dialogue and monologue in the passage.

d What is the reason for and the effect of the use of lines of capital letters?

e Note the form of the plural possessive *ladies'*. Give the plural possessive form for the following nouns:

    detective   agency   secretary   person   cattle

6

a Write adjectives of your own to describe the landscape and setting of Text 9B.

b Write adjectives of your own to describe the character of Mma Ramotswe's father.

c Make notes and write a half-page character sketch of Mma Ramotswe. Think about how the style of the passage contributes to the reader's impression of her character.

 Text 9C

Caped do-gooder takes Czech law enforcement into his own hands

He may not look much of a superhero in his blue tights, but a masked Czech vigilante who fights **antisocial** behaviour has found fame after posting videos of his *stunts* on YouTube.

The <u>self-styled saviour</u> <u>goes by the name of</u> Super Vaclav and hides his real identity in a mock Superman costume complete with a blue cape, a mask, a white ski helmet and black jump boots.

Somewhat overweight and <u>pushing 40</u>, Super Vaclav has become the *scourge* of Prague's drug dealers, dog foulers and inconsiderate drivers. Indeed, he targets almost anyone he regards as a **nuisance**, including **illicit** smokers, **graffiti** artists and residents who refuse to recycle their rubbish.

Videos of his *feats* include one showing him using a forklift truck to lift a Mini that has been wrongly parked in a disabled parking bay. He left the car suspended two metres above the ground until the *bemused* owner came back to claim it.

Other footage shows Super Vaclav following people who have dropped litter to make them return and put it in the bin.

There is also film of him blocking the traffic on one of Prague's busiest roads with a large banner urging motorists to protect the **environment** by walking or cycling to work instead.

Super Vaclav said his deeds were intended to inspire his fellow citizens to <u>civic action</u>. 'I think something is foul in this country and I'm frustrated because nobody will do anything about it. We're all passive and seem completely *indifferent*, <u>be it about</u> politics or anything else,' he said. 'I had no other choice but to put on a costume. I believe our country needs a superhero.'

Bojan Pancevski, *Sunday Times*

7 a Give synonyms for the following five words in italics in Text 9C:

stunts   scourge   feats   bemused   indifferent

b Look at the five bold words in the passage, which are difficult to spell, and then write them from memory using the LCWC (Look, Cover, Write, Check) method.

antisocial   nuisance   illicit   graffiti   environment

c Write the five underlined expressions in another way:

self-styled saviour   goes by the name of   pushing 40
civic action   be it about

8 Work in pairs for this activity.

a Argue whether or not people should take the law into their own hands, as in Text 9C. One of you argues Yes and the other No.

b Design a cartoon strip with speech bubbles to show a confrontation between Super Vaclav and a law breaker, then perform the dialogue to the class.

c Discuss with your partner the idea of superheroes, thinking of as many aspects of the topic as you can, and then contribute to a class discussion on the subject.

Text 9D is an abridged extract from a short story called 'The Destructors' in which a gang of teenage boys is persuaded by its new leader to commit a crime.

Text 9D

Next day T. astonished them all. He was late at the rendezvous, and the voting for that day's **exploit** took place without him. At Blackie's suggestion the gang was to **disperse** in pairs, take buses at random, and see how many free rides could be snatched from **unwary** conductors (the operation was to be carried out in pairs   5 to avoid cheating). They were drawing lots for their companions when T. arrived.

    'Where you been, T.?' Blackie asked. 'You can't vote now. You know the rules.'

    'I've been *there*,' T. said. He looked at the ground, as though   10 he had thoughts to hide.

    'Where?'

    'At Old Misery's.'

    'At Old Misery's?' Blackie said. There was nothing in the rules against it, but he had a sensation that T. was treading on   15 dangerous ground. He asked hopefully, 'Did you break in?'

'No. I rang the bell.'

'And what did you say?'

'I said I wanted to see his house.'

'What did he do?'

'He showed it me.'

'Pinch anything?'

'No.'

'What did you do it for then?'

The gang had gathered round: it was as though an **impromptu** court were about to form to try some case of **deviation**. T. said, 'It's a beautiful house,' and still watching the ground, meeting no one's eyes, he licked his lips first one way, then the other.

'What do you mean, a beautiful house?' Blackie asked with scorn.

'It's got a staircase two hundred years old like a corkscrew. Nothing holds it up.'

'What do you mean, nothing holds it up. Does it float?'

'It's to do with opposite forces, Old Misery said.'

'What else?'

'There's panelling. Two hundred years old.'

'Is Old Misery two hundred years old?'

Someone laughed suddenly and then was quiet again. The meeting was in a serious mood. For the first time since T. had strolled into the car-park and joined the gang on the first day of the school holidays his position was in danger. It only needed a single use of his real name and the gang would be at his heels. 40

'What did you do it for?' Blackie asked. He was just, he had no jealousy, he was anxious to retain T. in the gang if he could. It was the word 'beautiful' that worried him – that belonged to a class world that you could still see **parodied** by a man wearing a top hat and a monocle, with a haw-haw accent. He was tempted to say, 'My dear Trevor, old chap', and unleash his hell hounds. 'If you'd broken in,' he said sadly – that indeed would have been an exploit worthy of the gang. 45 50

'This was better,' T. said. 'I found out things.' He continued to stare at his feet, not meeting anybody's eye, as though he were absorbed in some dream he was unwilling – or ashamed – to share. 55

'What things?'

'Old Misery's going to be away all tomorrow and over the weekend.'

Blackie said with relief, 'You mean we could break in?' 60

'And pinch things?' somebody asked.

Blackie said, 'Nobody's going to pinch things. Breaking in – that's good enough, isn't it? We don't want any court stuff.'

'I don't want to pinch anything,' T. said. 'I've got a better idea.'

'What is it?' 65

T. raised his eyes, as grey and disturbed as the drab August day. 'We'll pull it down,' he said. 'We'll destroy it.'

Blackie gave a single hoot of laughter and then fell quiet, **daunted** by the serious **implacable** gaze.

'What'd the police be doing all the time?' he said. 70

'They'd never know. We'd do it from inside. I've found a way in.' He said with a sort of intensity, 'We'd be like worms, don't you see, in an apple. When we came out again there'd be nothing there, no staircase, no panels, nothing but just walls, and then we'd make the walls fall down – somehow.' 75

'We'd go to prison,' Blackie said.

'Who's to prove? And anyway we wouldn't have pinched anything.' He added without the smallest flicker of **glee**, 'There wouldn't be anything to pinch after we'd finished.'

'There wouldn't be time,' Blackie said. 'I've seen 80 housebreakers at work.'

'There are twelve of us,' T. said. 'We'd organise.'

'None of us know how—'

'I know,' T. said. He looked across at Blackie. 'Have you got a better plan?' 85

'The gang's got to vote.'

'Put it up then.'

Blackie said uneasily, 'It's proposed that tomorrow and Monday we destroy Old Misery's house.

'Who's in favour?' 90

T. said, 'It's carried.'

It was the end of Blackie's leadership. He went away to the back of the car-park and began to kick a stone, dribbling it this way and that. Beyond, paying no more attention to him than to a stranger, the gang had gathered round T. 95

Graham Greene, *The Destructors* (abridged)

9 Work in pairs to discuss Text 9D.

a Explain in each case the evidence for your inference.
  i Why do you think T. wants to destroy the house?
  ii What do you think Blackie will do next?
  iii How do you think the story will end?

 b The teacher will choose students to be in the 'hot seat' as the three characters from the story, and students in turn will ask them questions. First plan questions for hotseating each of the characters:
  i Old Misery
  ii Blackie
  iii Trevor (T.)

 Tip

For Activity 9b
Hotseating

Hotseating is a technique for exploring the thoughts and feelings, motivations and intentions, of a fictional character. When in the 'hot seat', the student imagines themselves as the character and infers from the text plausible answers to questions, trying to adopt the character's attitudes and even their way of speaking. The questioners try to get to the reasons for a character's behaviour and their views on the other characters, so, for instance, someone might ask Old Misery why he showed Trevor round his house and pointed out its architectural features to him. The reasons why Trevor plans the destruction of the house are not stated in the story, only implied.

c With a partner, choose one of the following pairs of characters and plan and practise a dialogue – to be performed to the class – which could have taken place between them at the end of the story after the house has been destroyed. Try to get into role and use as many ideas and quotations from the extract as you can. Think about setting and context, and how Trevor might talk differently to these three different kinds of people:
  i Trevor and Blackie
  ii Trevor and Old Misery
  iii Trevor and a police officer.

10 **a** Comment on the implications and connotations of the title of Text 9D.

b Write a news report of the demolition of Old Misery's House. Give it a headline, and make up names and addresses and any other facts as necessary.

c Write the next half page of the narrative, revealing what you think would happen next. Read it to the class and decide whose version is the most plausible and stylistically consistent.

Key point

Continuing a narrative

When asked to continue a piece of fiction, you should try to make it seem convincing by using the same style as the passage, as well as making the speech and behaviour of characters consistent with what has gone before. Look at the type of sentences, vocabulary and imagery that have been used so far, and continue to create the same atmosphere.

Text 9E is a complete (abridged) short story called 'A Hero'. American spellings have been used.

Text 9E

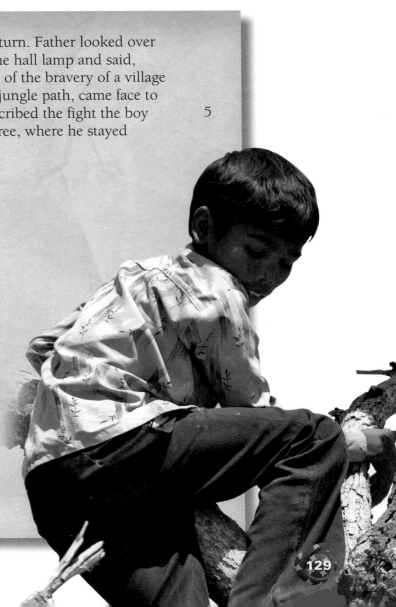

For Swami events took an unexpected turn. Father looked over the newspaper he was reading under the hall lamp and said, 'Swami, listen to this: "News is to hand of the bravery of a village lad who, while returning home by the jungle path, came face to face with a tiger ..."' The paragraph described the fight the boy had with the tiger and his **flight** up a tree, where he stayed for half a day till some people came that way and killed the tiger.

5

After reading it through, Father looked at Swami fixedly and asked, 'What do you say to that?'

Swami said, 'I think he must have been a very strong and grown-up person, not at all a boy. How could a boy fight a tiger?'

'You think you are wiser than the newspaper?' Father sneered. 'A man may have the strength of an elephant and yet be a coward: whereas another may have the strength of a straw, but if he has courage he can do anything. Courage is everything, strength and age are not important.'

Swami **disputed** the theory. 'How can it be, Father? Suppose I have all the courage, what can I do if a tiger should attack me?'

'Leave alone strength, can you prove you have courage? Let me see if you can sleep alone tonight in my office room.'

A frightful **proposition**, Swami thought. He had always slept beside his granny in the passage, and any change in this arrangement kept him trembling and awake all night. He hoped at first that his father was only joking. He mumbled weakly, 'Yes,' and tried to change the subject; he said very loudly and with a great deal of enthusiasm, 'We are going to admit even elders in our cricket club hereafter. We are buying brand-new bats and balls. Our captain has asked me to tell you ...'   30   35

'We'll see about it later,' Father cut in. 'You must sleep alone hereafter.' Swami realized that the matter had gone beyond his control: from a challenge it had become a plain command; he knew his father's **tenacity** at such moments.   40

'From the first of next month I'll sleep alone, Father.'

'No, you must do it now. It is disgraceful sleeping beside granny or mother like a baby. You are in the second form and I don't at all like the way you are being brought up,' he said, and looked at his wife, who was rocking the cradle. 'Why do you look at me while you say it?' she asked. 'I hardly know anything about the boy.'   45

'No, no, I don't mean you,' Father said.

'If you mean that your mother is spoiling him, tell her so; and don't look at me,' she said, and turned away.   50

Swami's father sat gloomily gazing at the newspaper on his lap. Swami rose silently and tiptoed away to his bed in the passage. Granny was sitting up in her bed, and remarked, 'Boy, are you already feeling sleepy? Don't you want a story?' Swami made wild **gesticulations** to silence his granny, but that good lady saw nothing. So Swami threw himself on his bed and pulled the blanket over his face.   55

Granny said, 'Don't cover your face. Are you really very sleepy?' Swami leant over and whispered, 'Please, please, shut up, granny. Don't talk to me, and don't let anyone call me even if the house is on fire. If I don't sleep at once I shall perhaps die ...' He turned over, curled, and snored under the blanket till he found his blanket pulled away.   60

Presently Father came and stood over him. 'Swami, get up,' he said. He looked like an **apparition** in the semi-darkness of the passage, which was lit by a cone of light from the hall. Swami stirred and groaned as if in sleep. Father said, 'Get up, Swami.' Granny pleaded, 'Why do you disturb him?'   65

'Get up, Swami,' he said for the fourth time, and Swami got up. Father rolled up his bed, took it under his arm, and said, 'Come with me.' Swami looked at his granny, hesitated for a moment,   70

and followed his father into the office room. On the way he threw a look of appeal at his mother and she said, 'Why do you take him to the office room? He can sleep in the hall, I think.'

'I don't think so,' Father said, and Swami slunk behind him with bowed head.   75

'Let me sleep in the hall, Father,' Swami pleaded. 'Your office room is very dusty and there may be scorpions behind your law books.'

'There are no scorpions, little fellow. Sleep on the bench if   80
you like.'

'Can I have a lamp burning in the room?'

'No. You must learn not to be afraid of darkness. It is only a question of habit. You must **cultivate** good habits.'

'Will you at least leave the door open?'

'All right. But promise you will not roll up your bed and go to your granny's side at night. If you do it, mind you, I will make you the <u>laughing-stock</u> of your school.'

Swami felt cut off from humanity. He was pained and angry. He didn't like the **strain** of cruelty he saw in his father's nature. He hated the newspaper for printing the tiger's story. He wished that the tiger hadn't spared the boy, who didn't appear to be a boy after all, but a monster....

As the night advanced and the silence in the house deepened, his heart beat faster. A ray of light from the street lamp strayed in and cast shadows on the wall. Through the stillness all kinds of noises reached his ears – the ticking of the clock, rustle of trees, snoring sounds, and some vague night insects humming.

Swami hurriedly got up and spread his bed under the bench and crouched there. It seemed to be a much safer place, more compact and reassuring. He shut his eyes tight and encased himself in his blanket once again and unknown to himself fell asleep, and in sleep was racked with nightmares. A tiger was chasing him. His feet stuck to the ground. He desperately tried to escape but his feet would not move; the tiger was at his back, and he could hear its claws scratch the ground ... scratch, scratch, and then a light thud....Swami tried to open his eyes, but his eyelids would not open and the nightmare continued. It threatened to continue forever. Swami groaned in despair.

With a desperate effort he opened his eyes. He put his hand out to feel his granny's presence at his side, as was his habit, but he only touched the wooden leg of the bench. And his lonely state came back to him. He sweated with fright. And now what was this rustling? He moved to the edge of the bench and stared into the darkness. Something was moving down. He lay gazing at it in horror. His end had come. As it came nearer he crawled out from under the bench, hugged it <u>with all his might</u>, and used his teeth on it like a **mortal** weapon.... 120

'Aiyo! Something has bitten me,' went forth an agonized, thundering cry and was followed by a heavy tumbling and falling amidst furniture.

In a moment Father, cook, and a servant came in, carrying light. 125

And all three of them fell on the burglar who lay amidst the furniture with a bleeding ankle....

Congratulations were showered on Swami next day. His classmates looked at him with respect, and his teacher patted his back. The headmaster said that he was a true scout. Swami had 130 bitten into the flesh of one of the most notorious house-breakers of the district and the police were grateful to him for it.

The Inspector said, 'Why don't you join the police when you are grown up?'

Swami said <u>for the sake of</u> politeness, 'Certainly, yes,' though 135 he had quite made up his mind to be an engine driver, a railway guard, or a bus conductor later in life.

When he returned home from the club that night, Father asked, 'Where is the boy?'

'He is asleep.' 140

'Already!'

'He didn't have a wink of sleep the whole of last night,' said his mother.

'Where is he sleeping?'

'In his usual place,' Mother said casually. 'He went to bed at 145 seven-thirty.'

'Sleeping beside his granny again!' Father said. 'No wonder he wanted to be asleep before I could return home – clever boy!'

Mother lost her temper. 'You let him sleep where he likes. You needn't risk his life again....' 150

Father mumbled as he went in to change: 'All right, **molly-coddle** and spoil him as much as you like. Only don't blame me afterwards....'

Swami, following the whole conversation from under the blanket, felt tremendously relieved to hear that his father was 155 giving him up.

R. K. Narayan

11 a Replace the ten words in bold in Text 9E with a synonym.

flight   disputed   proposition   tenacity   gesticulations
apparition   cultivate   strain   mortal   molly-coddle

b Rephrase in your own words the five underlined words and phrases.

Leave alone   hereafter   laughing-stock   with all his might
for the sake of

c Explain how ellipsis (...) is used in the passage for different purposes.

12 Read Text 9E aloud, with one person reading the part of the narrator and other people taking the different roles. Work in small groups on Text 9E to prepare answers to the following questions for class discussion.

a What is the story apparently about? What is its subtext (i.e. what is it really about)?

b What is ironic about the story and its title?

c Which characters is the reader sympathetic to and which not? Give reasons in each case.

d Comment on the opening of the story.

e Comment on the ending of the story.

Text 9F is a complete (abridged) futuristic short story called 'Visitors'.

Text 9F

She saw the mini-bus pass the kitchen window before pulling up on the gravel driveway to the side of the house. It looked like a tradesman's van, with metal panels where the windows would normally be, and ladders strapped to the roof racks. But there was no company name on the side of the van, and she felt   5
her stomach tighten at the unfairness of it. Not again; not so soon!

The knocking was confident but not intimidating. Civilised. She opened the door. There were three men standing on the porch.

Two wore clean, neat, blue overalls with official **insignia** on   15
the pockets. The third man, who had knocked at the door, had
a lighter build. He wore a *conservative* two-piece suit and was
approaching middle age. There was a professional, competent
air about him. He looked thoroughly respectable.

'Yes?' she asked.   20

'Morning, madam,' he replied **affably**. 'This is a robbery.'

Inside the house, she led them to the lounge. They followed
politely, conscious of their movements.

'We had a team through only two weeks ago,' she
complained.   25

'Not one of ours, madam. I'm afraid we can't cooperate with
the other firms. Competition, you know. You can always put in a
complaint.'

'Well, where do you want to start?'

'We'd like to put you in the picture first,' replied the leader,   30
taking a small notebook from his suit pocket. 'We like our
customers to know they are dealing with professional people,
so I'll just run through the basics.' He flipped through the
alphabetical tabs on the side of the book, opened to a page
covered in neat, pencilled notes and diagrams. He read from   35
it in a confirmatory tone, pausing now and then to check that
she understood the details and was happy, 'Mrs Morrison,
42 Wentworth ...' She nodded; he went on. 'Now, we've
disconnected your phone at the junction on the corner, and
we have a man in the street with a second vehicle just to make   40
sure we won't be surprised by anything unexpected.' He gave
a small, proud smile. 'We disconnected your power on arrival,
and of course we'll put that back on as we leave. We know how
inconvenient it is to have freezers defrost and so on. The phone,
however, is your responsibility as always. We know that your   45
daughter is at work and won't be back until four at the earliest.
We also know that she usually telephones you at eleven, so that
it will be ...' he checked his watch, briskly, '... two and a half
hours before she notices the disconnection. Plenty of time. We
have, of course, checked out your deliveries, none of which are   50
due this morning.' He paused before flipping the notebook shut.

'Yes,' she said politely. 'You seem very thorough. You must
have spent some time checking.'

'Two weeks is our normal time frame,' he said, finally closing
the pad. 'A bit unfortunate for you really that we didn't see the   55
other firm come through. It must have been a little over two
weeks ago that they called.'

'Yes.'

The next was asked a little anxiously, as though the wrong answer might introduce a note of unpleasantness. 'Did they leave much?' 60

'Uh, no. They took the lot. But we got the insurance people right away so we've been able to replace most of it.'

The man was clearly relieved. 'Oh good. We hate having to extract a *forfeit*.' 65

'What is it at the moment?'

'Windows this month,' he replied, signalling to one of the other two men, who had been standing patiently by the window. 'Of course, we break them from the inside so as not to get glass on the furnishings. Well then! We'd better get to work.' 70

Presently, all three men returned to the lounge. Disregarding her for the moment, the leader spoke to his men. 'Bring the stuff here and we'll make up the inventory as we load it into the van. It'll be more efficient that way.'

The two **accomplices** nodded and set to work. A small pile of 75 goods began to build near the entrance hall. Television set; DVD recorder; kitchen appliances; some jewellery. It didn't take long.

He turned to the woman. 'Will you accompany me on the inspection? We won't entertain claims unless they are notified immediately.' 80

Reluctantly she followed him from room to room, casting a sad glance at the stack of appliances on the floor. She had to admit that it was a very professional job. Except for the goods they had taken, everything was in its place. Despite herself, she had to remark on the fact. 85

'Well, we do have standards to maintain,' said the man. 'People still remember the old days – a brick through the window, contents strewn about. Mainly it was kids back then, *amateurs*. People felt as if their homes had been violated, as if they weren't safe any more. But things have changed so much 90 since the new **legislation**. We have to be accredited, audited. It puts the operation on a whole new level.'

'Even so,' she replied. 'I think we'd be better off without... Look, you've done a very good job, and you've a right to be proud of it, but I just don't see that it's really necessary.' 95

'You're talking about jobs, madam, people's livelihood. The country couldn't handle the unemployment. Nationalising robbery was the best thing the government could do in the circumstances.'

It took only a few minutes for them to transfer the haul 100 to the van. They left her with a copy of the list for insurance purposes. She was only half way through checking it when a car

flashed past the window and skidded to a halt on the gravel. Its doors fell open, *disgorging* a **motley** collection of young men. There were four of them, dirty, *unkempt*, and hardly into their teens. They pounded up the steps onto the porch and hammered at the door, rattling the frosted glass. She opened the door. The eldest leered at her, grinned, and announced himself. 'Police, Mrs Morrison. Understand you've been robbed.'

110

Brian Moon

13
a Use the five bold words in the passage in sentences which show their meaning as used in the story.

insignia   affably   accomplices   legislation   motley

b Give the opposites of the five words in italics in the passage:

conservative   forfeit   amateurs   disgorging   unkempt

c Turn the story into a mini-saga of exactly 50 words. Use the tip below to help you.

For Activity 13c
Mini-sagas

A mini-saga is a narrative and is therefore in a different style from a summary of the story, which is informative writing in which there is no need to consider use of speech, tension, structure, word order, climax, irony or any other devices which one expects in a narrative, however short. In order to reduce the length to exactly 50 words, having removed any unnecessary information or description, consider the following ways:
- hyphenation where possible
- replacing phrasal verbs with one-word synonyms
- using a semi-colon instead of a connective
- using active rather than passive verb forms
- avoiding simple sentences (each needing a subject).

14 a Explain the 'unfairness' that Mrs Morrison experiences in Text 9F.

b Explain what would have happened if Mrs Morrison's house had not contained appliances and valuables.

c Write and read out the one-page letter of complaint that Mrs Morrison sends to the Minister for Employment.

15 a Contribute to a list of all the ironies in Text 9F, including the title.

b Say whether you think the situation and events in the story could ever really happen, and justify your opinion.

c Give your opinion to the class on whether you enjoyed this story more or less than the prevous ironic short story in this unit, Text 9E, explaining your reasons.

16 You are going to plan and write an ironic short story which concerns a crime and/or a hero. Remember that a good short story usually has only two or three main characters (who may use dialogue), deals with one event, and ends with a twist or surprise in the final sentence.

- Collect some ideas (you may wish to think of stories or films you know).

- Consider them and choose the best.

- Make a plan.

- Draft your story.

- Give it a suitable title.

- Produce a final version.

- Swap it with a partner and correct any errors.

- Give it to your teacher.

UNIT 10 All in a day's work

This unit looks at informal versus formal language, prefixes, indirect speech and phrasal and prepositional verbs. Reader positioning and inferential reading are considered. You will compare poems, looking at their sound and imagery, and write a formal letter, a work journal, and a monologue.

Activities

1 Make notes on the following, for class discussion.

a Which do you think is the most difficult or most unpleasant job?

b How do you think modern jobs differ from traditional ones?

c What work do you want to do when you finish your education?

Text 10A is about Mark Pennington, a driller at Kalgoorlie's Super Pit, Australia's largest open-pit gold mine.

I **get up** at twenty past four. I tend to wake before the alarm <u>goes off</u>, so I flick it off so as not to wake *my missus*. Breakfast is tea and toast with jam and Vegemite, then *I'm off*.

The drive to work is 45 kilometres east across the bush. It's in the heart of Western Australia's goldfields and most days there are no kangaroos, just the rising sun and a lot of traffic coming the other way – mainly *night-shift blokes* heading home from my pit in Kalgoorlie.

I'm there at 5.45 and I tag in at the gatehouse, then **get changed**. I chat to my cross mate <u>going off</u> the night shift. We each operate 10-hour shifts, with a four-hour break between them, and this is our only chance to <u>bring up</u> issues and discuss *where we're at*.

I *grab my gear*, jump into my **Ute** and drive down through the portal, which is like entering a different universe. I'm a jumbo operator, and a jumbo is a sit-in mobile drill with two mechanical arms sticking out in front to **get hold of** the rock face, and a big four-metre-long drill bit to mine the gold.

It's a 15-minute drive to where we start – 500 metres underground. I **get to** the rock face and plug in a trailing cable – a long extension on a reel. We use hydraulic drills to dampen down the dust, so water is pumping when you drill, and running past you. Depending on the ground we're working, it takes a minute or two to drill a hole. My drill-rig produces a lot of heat, so if it's hot outside, it can **get up to** 50 degrees down here. It's extremely noisy, so I have foam earplugs and earmuffs. Without hearing protection, you risk instant, permanent hearing loss.

Lunch is at midday, and while we **get** half an hour, I usually take just 15 minutes. Most days, it's a long white roll with cheese, egg and chutney that I bring in myself.

I've been here for 20 years now, and in that time, mining **has got** very industrialised. But it goes on being dangerous. *I've lost people* underground ... good mates.

The end of my day is at 3.45, because the controlled explosions take place then. So everyone is tagged out and goes off so that the blast crew can fire dynamite at the mine face. The rock is then crushed and goes through a long process at the mill to **get the gold out**. Before I leave, I shower to **get rid of** the dust and clock out. I'm home *by 5-ish* and once I'm inside I feel like *I'm the king of my castle*.

I actually started my working life as a **jackaroo** on a large sheep station, then I did maintenance on grain silos in the **wheat belt**. I also had a fishing business with *my old man* in Adelaide as an **abalone** diver. I'd dive down 30 metres, 10 hours a day, with just hook-up air from the surface. It was dangerous. As well as the threat of sharks, I'd often come up coughing blood, having torn my lung tissue. I think it's what attracted me to mining. It sounds masochistic, but danger makes me feel like I'm putting in a hard day's work ... it makes me feel alive that I **get to go** so deep.

I watch TV and go to bed about 9, and before I turn off the light I might read a bit. *I love sci-fi*, but as imaginative as the stories might be, I still have a very real alternative universe to return to when I wake up again.

Sunday Times Magazine

Ute	abbreviation for utility vehicle or pick-up truck
jackaroo	farm worker
wheat belt	one of the nine regions of Western Australia; farmland where corn is grown
abalone	shellfish considered a delicacy, with a mother-of-pearl shell made into jewellery

2
a Write the ten words or phrases in italics in Text 10A in more formal language.

b The passage uses phrasal verbs with *bring* and *go*, which are underlined. List as many others as you can think of. Give synonyms for each.

c Infer and explain the meanings of the following five prefixes or word stems as used in the passage, and give examples of other words which begin with these:

per   hydr   dyna   alter   uni

Tip

For Activity 2c
Word stems and prefixes

A stem is a meaningful word or part of a word (also known as a root word, or morpheme in American English) which cannot be divided and which can have affixes (prefixes or suffixes) attached to it, e.g. *change* and *gen* (which can become *interchangeably* and *regenerate* when both prefix and suffixes are added). A stem can also be added to another stem to make a compound word, e.g. *kilo/metre*, *photo/graphy*, *psycho/logical*. These are often scientific words or those which come from Greek. In the list in Activity 2c, *hydr*, *dyna* and *alter* are word stems.

A prefix has a generic not a specific meaning, can be attached to a range of words, and cannot exist alone. In the list in Activity 2c, *per* and *uni* are prefixes.

3 **a** Give the verb form of the following five nouns in Text 10A. Be careful with the spelling:

extension   loss   explosion   maintenance   threat

b Replace the ten uses of the verb 'get', used in the passage in bold, with more formal verbs.

c **i** Without looking at the passage until you have answered the question, complete the ten prepositional verbs used.
ii Where the verbs can be used with other prepositions, give the alternatives.

tend _____   clock _____
chat _____   attracted _____
dampen _____   turn _____
depending _____   return _____
fire _____   wake _____

Key point

Prepositional and phrasal verbs

Prepositional verbs are those which are always followed by the same preposition or pair of prepositions, e.g. to *wait for* something, to *clock in/out*, or where the preposition is a literal position, e.g. to *turn around*, to *go back*. The preposition may not immediately follow the verb, as in 'he *aimed* the arrow *at* the target'.

Phrasal verbs are idiomatic expressions, often using common verbs such as *take*, *come* and *put*, formed with different prepositions to create new verbs with distinct meanings, e.g. *to take up* something, where the meaning of the preposition(s) is not a literal reference to place. They can be transitive or intransitive (i.e. take an object or not). The preposition becomes an adverb when it is made part of a phrasal verb, as it is no longer describing position. Some phrasal verbs can take two prepositions/adverbs, such as *look forward to*, *put up with*.

Text 10B is an extract from a novel set in India. Lila and her sisters have called the medicine-man in the hope that he will cure their sick mother.

Text 10B

At the hut there was nothing to do but wait.

At last they heard the throbbing of the drum and the long eerie blasts on the trumpet which meant the medicine-man was near. He was preceded by the little dwarf cow that he dressed in tassels and necklaces of beads, with an embroidered cloth covering her hump.

He raised his hand in the air as he marched over the log on the creek and gave another long blast on his trumpet which was made of bone. The bone of what? the girls wondered uneasily.

Lila came running out of the house to speak to the medicine-man.

'My mother is ill. She has been ill for a long time. Now she has fever too. Have you any medicine for fever? Have you any medicine for making her strong? She is so weak,' Lila explained.

'Slowly, slowly, daughter. What is the hurry? First, I must have water for my cow – fresh well water. Next, I must have grass for her. Fresh, tender grass. Then I will come and see your mother.'

So that was how things had to be done. After the cow had been looked after, he too demanded attention. Lila had to heat a tumbler of tea for him which he sipped, sitting on a string cot under the frangipani tree while the girls stood before him and told him how their mother was growing weaker and weaker, refusing to eat and unable to get up at all. 'And now she is hot with fever,' Lila wailed suddenly, no longer able to speak calmly.

The man looked at her with his sharp, bright eyes, understanding how it was with her. He got up quickly and started being very busy. To their surprise he did not go in to see their mother as they had expected he would. Instead, he ordered them to build a fire on the threshold of the hut. Once it had started crackling and smoking, he flung in packets of

flowers that he took from a bag slung over the cow's back – jasmine and marigold, hibiscus and frangipani.

When the fire had died down, he poked at it with a long stick, scattering the ashes so that they cooled. Then he scooped them up into his cupped hand and asked for water. They brought him a tumbler and he poured a little into the palm of his hand and with one thumb and forefinger he mixed it with the ash. Then he went in to see their mother at last.

The man told her to open her mouth and put out her tongue, which she did, and on it he dropped some of the ash. 'Eat, sister,' he said. 'Holy ash, purified ash. It will purify you within. It will drive away the demons that create the fever. Swallow.' He kept rolling small balls of ash between his fingers and dropping them into her mouth, making her swallow them. Then he clapped his hands together, broke into the loud recitation of prayers, and walked out.

The girls followed, dazed.

Lifting his trumpet, the medicine-man blew a long blast on it; he stared down into their faces and looked very fierce. 'So?' he shouted at them. 'What do you do now? Stare at my face? Got nothing to give me but your stares? Think I can fill my stomach with that? Think I do it all for free?'

Lila shook herself guiltily and ran into the hut, knowing there was no money. But she came out with something in her hand – the ring their mother used to wear when she was well and that she had taken off and kept behind the mirror on the shelf now that she was ill. It was of silver – rather blackened and twisted now, but still silver. The girls gave a gasp of astonishment, but the man merely snatched it out of Lila's hand, tucked it away into one of his pouches and marched off towards his cow without a word of thanks.

Anita Desai, *The Village by the Sea*

4 **a** As brief notes in your own words, give the stages of the visit of the medicine-man in Text 10B.

    b **i** Quote the words and phrases in the passage that make the medicine-man unsympathetic to the reader.
       ii Write a sentence giving your impression of him.

    c **i** Quote the words and phrases in the passage that make Lila sympathetic to the reader.
       ii Write a sentence giving your impression of her.

For Activities 4b and 4c
Sympathy and empathy

The reader is positioned in fiction – and sometimes in non-fiction texts too – to respond to a character either sympathetically or unsympathetically, i.e. with affection and approval, or not. This is achieved through their actions, their attitudes, and the way they speak. The situation they are in and the way they treat the other characters are also significant in the reader's formation of an opinion about them.

    Empathy is the ability to understand and share the feelings of another, and readers are expected to possess this quality and to demonstrate it in their responses to fiction texts. When you are asked to write an empathic response to a literary work, in the first person as one of the characters, you need to try to adopt their way of thinking and feeling, and even some of their speech habits, to show that you are able to identify with them.

5 Discuss the following questions as a class, giving evidence in each case to support your inferences.

    a Why do you think the medicine-man in Text 10B holds such an important position in his district?

    b What do you think is the significance of the cow in the passage?

    c Do you think the medicine-man is likely to have been successful in curing the mother?

    d Why do you think her sisters gasp when Lila brings out her mother's ring?

    e What do you think 'understanding how it was with her' means?

Text 10C is the work experience diary of a 16-year-old girl in New Zealand, written as a school assignment.

Monday

My mum drove me the 60 kilometres to the heliport at Rotorua. We had to report by 7am, so that meant a very early start! But I hardly slept all night anyway, as I was so excited. They waved us through security, and I was really worried as we drove up to the hangar – what if it had all been a misunderstanding, if they laughed at me when I said I was there to work with them for a week? It was really difficult to arrange this work experience; my friends have all gone to sit in offices and are just making the coffee, and I wanted more than that. But it was all right. Kevin in the office said 'Hi', they were expecting me, but was I up for some hard work? You bet I was! Was my stomach strong? I hoped so.

HeliVetNZ is a unique company, and my first duty was to attend an orientation briefing where they explained the services they offered. Here in NZ many farms are up in the mountains and it's really hard for vets to get there fast enough when there's an emergency. So HeliVet has a team of highly experienced vets on standby, and when the call comes, out they go!

Actually, there were no callouts today, so I was able to meet the team and begin to understand how it all worked. They let me sit in the helicopter!

Tuesday

The callout came before 8am. We ran to the helicopter, the pilot, the vet, the loadmaster and me. I was taking the place of the flying nurse. It was a big responsibility. You don't know where you're going until you're in the air. It all comes through on the radio from the control room. There was a cow in labour on a high farm and they couldn't deliver the calf. If you don't get there quickly enough the calf can get tangled up in the umbilical cord (IGCSE Biology!) and asphyxiate, so it's always a run to the helicopter and a rush to get into the air as fast as we can.

The loadmaster sits next to the pilot and they have to identify the farm from the air, which wasn't easy – there are so many up there – but somehow they managed it. We landed in a field next to the house, and three of us ran in while the pilot stayed in the helicopter. The farmer was waiting anxiously and took us to a barn. Jo, the vet, immediately took over, giving us all instructions. Helping a cow to calve turns out not to be a very subtle process – she stuck her hand inside the cow, and after a while attached a rope. The loadmaster and I pulled on the rope like a tug of war while Jo coaxed from within, and a minute later the calf plopped out! The calf was soon staggering around and we were back in the helicopter and on our way home, feeling we'd done a good job: a happy, groggy calf, a relieved mom and a very relieved farmer.

Wednesday

This was quite a boring day. No calls at all. I was itching to be flying into the mountains again, but instead I spent the time checking the medical supplies and polishing the helicopter. A helicopter is very big and there's an awful lot of metal to polish! It's not all drama like on TV, but I hope tomorrow will be a bit more lively…

Thursday

Today was pretty much a re-run of Tuesday – it's calving season and apparently it's common for the farmer to need help with difficult births. This time it was over before we got there, and everything was fine, but you never know, and the team always responds to a call just in case.

Friday

My last day. I was hoping for a really 'good' callout, and I was not disappointed! Apparently, a bunch of lambs had fallen into a gully in the mountains – that's the trouble with lambs, where one goes all the others will follow, no matter how crazy.

We were flying over really wild mountains. There was no way we could land anywhere. I couldn't see how we would ever even find them, but then I saw a green flare rising into the sky like a reversed comet, and we saw a group of men with a 4×4. This is where it got really scary. The loadmaster strapped Jo into a harness, and then she sat in the open door of the helicopter – and jumped out! But the winch is strong and these guys really know what they're doing. She was lowered slowly into the gully, while the pilot hovered really skilfully, frighteningly close to a cliff-face. I could see Jo scoop up a struggling lamb and tie it into the tiny stretcher she had, and then another.

She had to go down three times before they were all rescued and in the helicopter. As soon as she was out of the harness, Jo said 'They all need checking out. Take them all back.' So I helped her to look after the lambs, holding them as she sedated them, during the short flight back. She took them into the medical facility at the back of the hangar, but she said she thought they'd all recover once the shock had passed.

And that was it. I had to say goodbye and go home. But one thing I now know for sure: this is the only job I want to do!

6　**a** Describe the job of a helicopter vet, as described in Text 10C, in one sentence.

　　b What are the characteristics of informal spoken English that you notice in the passage?

　　c **i** Join the first four sentences in Tuesday's entry into one complex sentence.
　　　　ii Turn the following indirect speech below into direct speech:
　　　　She said she thought they'd all recover once the shock had passed.

7　**a** On a copy of Text 10C, underline in three colours the content which is narrative, reflective and informative in the entries for Monday and Friday.

　　b Write a formal letter to a company near where you live, asking them to allow you to do unpaid work during the next school holiday because you are interested in doing that kind of job when you leave school. Remember to use a polite and formal register for writing to people you don't know and wish to impress.

　　c Write a week's diary for your current school week. Talk about what you do each day and why, and how you feel about it, and include what other people do and say as well. First read the key point on the next page.

Key point

Diaries and journals

If the purpose of a diary is to record a particular event or series of events, such as a trip or other special experience, and it is written for others to read or as an official document, then it has the status of a journal or formal diary. This differs from a personal diary in that it is written in full sentences and an appropriately clear style to enable a reader to understand the content, even though it may contain some colloquial expression. Journals and formal diaries may be used as texts or set as tasks in exams, whereas personal diaries are not likely to be called for, since they are typically written in an informal register which includes abbreviations, jargon, exaggerated punctuation, fashionable expressions and non-sentences.

Text 10D is a poem about an area in Singapore. It uses American spelling of 'stories'.

Text 10D

Bukit Timah, Singapore

This highway I know,
the only way into the city
where the muddy canal goes.
These are the sides of coarse grasses
where the schoolboys stumble in early morning
wet-staining their white shoes.

This is the way the city is fed
men, machines,
flushed out of their short dreams
and suburban holes
to **churn** down this waiting **gullet**.
They flow endlessly this way
from dawn, before sky opens,

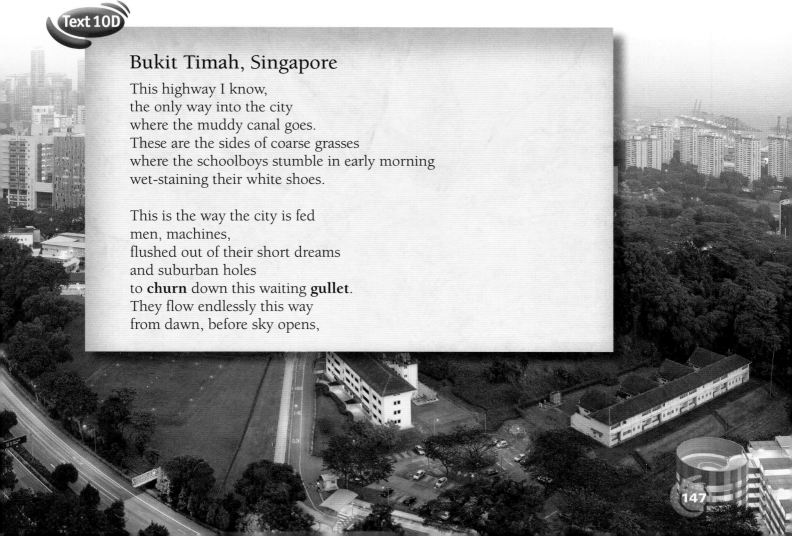

to the narrow glare of noon
and evening's slow closing.

Under the steaming morning,
ambition flashes by in a new car:
the reluctant salesman faced
with another day of selling his pride
hunches over the **lambretta**, swerving
from old farmer with fruit-heavy basket.
The women back from market
remark that this monsoon will be bad
for the price of vegetables:
their loitering children, too small for school,
learn the value of five cents, ten cents,
from hunger and these market days.

All morning the tired buses whine
their **monotonous** route, drag
from stop to stop,
disgorge schoolchildren, pale-faced clerks,
long-suffering civil servants,
pretty office girls, to feed
the **megalopolitan** appetite.

This highway I know,
the only way out of the city:
the same highway under the moon,
the same people under the sea-green
of lamps newly turned on at evening.

One day there will be tall buildings
here, where the green trees reach
for the narrow canal.
The holes where the restless sleepers are
will be neat, boxed up in ten-stories.
Life will be orderly, comfortable,
exciting, occasionally, at the new nightclubs.

I wonder what that old farmer would say
if he lived to come this way.

Lee Tzu Pheng

| lambretta | a type of motor scooter |

148

8 Work in a small group and present your answers to the class.

a Look up the following five words in bold in Text 10D and choose the best synonyms for the context:

churn gullet monotonous disgorge megalopolitan

b Comment on the imagery of the poem.

c Comment on the use of sound in the poem.

d Comment on the layout/line length of the poem.

e What would the old farmer say if he lived to come this way?

f What is the message of the poem?

MASTER KISHAN: WORLD'S YOUNGEST DIRECTOR

At ten, Kishan Shrikanth (aka Master Kishan) won a place in the book of Guinness World Records as the youngest director of a professional feature film. He gave this interview at the age of 12, by which time he had also acted in 26 movies. He lives in Bangalore, India.

If I am going to school, I wake up at 7.30. If I have other work – acting or directing – it might be earlier. In a month, I will be at least ten days in my school, and the other 20 or so days on my shoot. As soon as I get up, I go to bow at my parents' feet; that is the Indian sentiment. I drink water and go to the bathroom: brushing my teeth, washing my face, nature's call. I have breakfast with my sister, Kiran, who is nine. We have chocolate cornflakes, or omelette and a glass of milk.

When I was small, my dad would make videos of me playing. He would link the camera to the TV, so that I saw if I gave this reaction, I would look like this or that. I liked it very much. I was in fashion shows when I was three. A year later a friend of my dad's chose me for his movie *Grama Devathe* [The Village God, 2001]. It was made in Kannada, which is my mother tongue, and I played a boy with rich parents.

On the days I go to school I start at 8.30. I go to Camlin English School. I am often called a child prodigy. There is one child at my school, a genius who plays keyboards. And a very small boy who knows everything about 500 cars. I am learning English, science, maths, social studies, Kannada. We play football, volleyball, basketball and cricket. If I have won an award, my friends see the movie and give me their reports. Otherwise, everybody is very normal. My sister goes to the same school. She always comes first in dancing and singing, but she doesn't want to be in a film. She wants to be a doctor. I enjoy being onstage.

At 12 we start lunch. It's whatever my mum sends: pizza or noodles, or lemon rice and *sambar* [lentil and vegetable stew] and chapatti. In the afternoon we have more lessons, and general knowledge, computer science and free play. At 3.30 I get the bus home with my best friend, Suhas. Whatever I've missed in lessons, I pick up from him.

If there is homework I will do it, then Kiran and I play together. If there is any work, such as film-editing or designing, I go to the editing suite in our house.

I learnt how to direct on film shoots. I would watch my directors and ask them about a scene, and they would explain it to me. I talked to the cameraman and I began learning how the equipment works. The idea for the first film I directed, *Care of Footpath*, came to me when I was six. I saw homeless children on the streets selling newspapers to earn money as they had no parents. I felt bad. I wrote a story about it, and my father's friends read it and felt I should direct it. So I did the story outline and some Bangalore journalists did the screenplay. Today the government gives free food and education to children, but slum children still do not study. I hope the film encourages them to go to school. The film took about 60 days to shoot, and my parents were the producers. It was made in Kannada, and has been dubbed into Hindi, Tamil and Bengali. In June it won the jury prize at a children's film festival in Italy.

It's not hard working with big stars who are in my film; I might act and show them what I want. But directing isn't the same as acting; when I am directing it is a very long day. One day I started at 4am and ended at 3am the next day. I wasn't tired. I've got lots and lots of energy. We are now in pre-production on my second feature film, which is about cricket.

My parents don't let me go out alone because I get mobbed. But I am not shy. I'm happy people want to talk to me and ask for my autograph. In the afternoons I watch TV, and I like cartoons – *Tom and Jerry*, *Looney Tunes*, *Bugs Bunny* – and all kinds of movies: thriller, action, Bollywood, Hollywood, Italian...

I have a manager who organises my programme, but my parents accept all my movies for me, and guide me. They look after the money. I don't care for money. You should have a very rich heart, then you have a very rich human. We are Hindu and we go to the temple when we can. We worship Ganesha, the elephant god. My religion is humanity. I think everybody should be treated as human beings first.

The earliest I go to bed is 11pm, but normally it's 12. I don't like sleeping. Before I sleep I have some milk. Then I go to my parents' feet.

Sunday Times Magazine

9 Make notes on the following for class discussion.

a In what ways is Kishan in Text 10E a typical 12-year-old?

b In what ways is Kishan's life unusual?

c In what ways does Kishan's monologue show that he is only 12 years old?

10 Work with a partner for this activity.

a Rewrite using complex sentences the penultimate paragraph of Text 10E, in order to sound like a more mature speaker.

b Explain in one sentence for each how the following people might view Kishan:
  i his parents
  ii his friend Suhas
  iii the people who mob him in the street and ask for his autograph.

c Make up some questions that you would ask Master Kishan if you were a journalist interviewing him after reading the passage.

Text 10F

Carpet-weavers, Morocco

The children are at the loom of another world.
Their braids are oiled and black, their dresses bright.
Their assorted heights would make a melodious chime.

They watch their flickering knots like television.
As the garden of Islam grows, the bench will be raised.
Then they will lace the dark-rose veins of the tree-tops.

The carpet will travel in the merchant's truck.
It will be spread by the servants of the mosque.
Deep and soft, it will give when heaped with prayer.

The children are hard at work in the school of days.
From their fingers the colours of all-that-will-be fly
and freeze into the frame of all-that-was.

Carol Rumens

11 In small groups, discuss the poem in Text 10F.

a What is the situation being described in the poem?

b Which phrases in the poem do you consider effective, and why?

c What do you think the last verse of the poem is saying?

d What is the effect of the long, end-stopped lines of the poem?

e What do you think is ironic about the poem?

Monologue

I like working near a door. I like to have my work-bench close by, with a locker handy.

Here, the cold creeps in under the big doors, and in the summer hot dust swirls, clogging the nose. When the big doors open to admit a lorry-load of steel, conditions do not improve. Even so, I put up with it, and wouldn't care to shift to another bench, away from the big doors.

As one may imagine this is a noisy place with smoke rising, machines thumping and thrusting, people kneading, shaping, and putting things together. Because I am nearest to the big doors I am the farthest away from those who have to come down to shout instructions in my ear.

I am the first to greet strangers who drift in through the open doors looking for work. I give them as much information as they require, direct them to the offices, and acknowledge the casual recognition that one worker signs to another.

I can always tell the look on the faces of the successful ones as they hurry away. The look on the faces of the unlucky I know also, but cannot easily forget.

I have worked here for fifteen months.
It's too good to last.
Orders will fall off

and there will be a reduction in staff.
More people than we can cope with
will be brought in from other lands:
people who are also looking
for something more real, more lasting,
more permanent maybe, than dying . . . .
I really ought to be looking for another job
Before the axe falls.

These thoughts I push away, I think that I am lucky
to have a position by the big doors which open out
to a short alley leading to the main street; console
myself that if the worst happened I at least
would have no great distance to carry my gear and tool-box
off the premises.

I always like working near a door. I always look for a
work-bench hard by – in case an earthquake
occurs and fire breaks out, you know?

                                            Hone Tuwhare

12 Work with a partner.

    a Give your impressions, with supporting quotations, of the following aspects of Text 10G:
       i the job being described in the poem
       ii the time and place in which the poem is set
       iii the character of the speaker of the poem.

    b What do you think makes this text verse rather than prose?

    c What do Texts 10F and 10G have in common, and how do they differ?

13 Write a monologue in the role of someone at work engaged in their job. First make notes about the things they will describe around them and the tasks they are performing. Then write a draft, concentrating on giving it a distinctive voice. Use the tip below to help you.

For Activity 13
Writing a monologue

Monologues are more engaging and seem more authentic if they have an individual voice. There is a strong personal voice in each of the monologue texts in this unit, creating sympathy and empathy in the reader. (Empathy is the ability to understand and share the feelings of a real or fictional character.) It is also important to establish a sense of time and place, and an age and gender for the speaker.

    An idiolect is the speech habits peculiar to a particular person, i.e. a use of vocabulary and syntax that distinguishes them from other speakers. An idiolect may be an accent or a dialect (a particular form of the language which is peculiar to a specific region or social group). You could try writing your monologue in your local dialect of English.

UNIT 11 Wings and wheels

This unit looks at prefixes, connectives, hyphens, direct and indirect speech, and idioms. You will collate texts, make notes, do research, compose verse and draw a cartoon strip. Written responses will be a biography, a leaflet, an account, a review and a news report.

Activities

1 **a** Do you think it is of benefit to humanity that technology is constantly being used to make things perform and travel faster?

b What do you think is the attraction of speed?

c Give examples of how speed has become an obsession.

El Maestro

Juan Manuel Fangio (24 June 1911–17 July 1995), nicknamed El Maestro (the master) and El Chueco (the bow-legged one), was an Argentinian racing-car driver who dominated the first decade of Formula One racing.

From an early age he neglected his studies to pursue auto mechanics. In 1938 he entered his first national event, competing in a Ford V8. In 1940, he competed with a Chevrolet to win the Grand Prix International Championship, and thereafter devoted his time to the Argentine Turismo Carretera, becoming its champion and successfully defending his title a year later. He achieved further success competing in Europe in the late 1940s.

During the 1950s Fangio won five Formula One World Drivers' Championships – a record which stood for 46 years until beaten by Michael Schumacher – with four different teams (Alfa Romeo, Ferrari, Mercedes-Benz and Maserati). This feat has never been repeated. Furthermore, his record-breaking four wins in the Argentine Grand Prix earned Fangio the status of the only Argentine driver to have won on home soil. Regarded by many as one of the greatest F1 drivers of all time, his winning percentage of 46% (having won 24 of the 52 Formula One races he entered) is the highest ever.

Fangio became the honorary president of Mercedes-Benz Argentina in 1987, a post he retained until his death in 1995. A museum dedicated to him stands in the neighbourhood in which he was born and in 2011, on the centenary of his birth, tributes were paid around the world to remember his legacy.

Text 11B

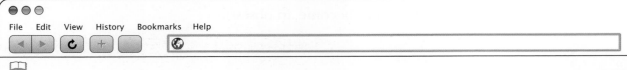

Some regard Juan Manuel Fangio as the greatest racing driver ever. He set records that are unlikely ever to be beaten. He began his career in races thousands of miles long across rough roads in South America. Only later in life, when he was in his forties, did he turn to Formula One and become equally successful there, winning his first title in 1951. He proved his observation and multi-tasking skills in Monaco in 1950, when he avoided ploughing into the wreckage of an invisible crash scene on the harbour road by noticing that the crowd were all looking at something around the corner and not at him, even though he was leading.

Afterwards he said, 'I was lucky. There had been a similar accident in 1936 and I happened to see a photograph of it the day before the race. As I came out of the chicane, I was aware of something different about the crowd – and then I remembered the photograph and braked as hard as I could.'

Formula One history was made by Fangio in the 1957 German Grand Prix, where he produced probably the greatest racing performance ever. It took place at the Nurburgring, the 14-mile track through the Eifel mountains which is considered to be the most challenging race circuit ever devised. Fangio became world champion for the fifth time and retired, aged 47, at the end of that racing season. He returned home to his birthplace, Balcarce, in order to manage a Mercedes car dealership. He was subsequently appointed president of Mercedes-Benz Argentina in 1974. He occasionally returned to Europe in later life to demonstrate his former racing cars. He also made a trip to the 1993 Brazilian Grand Prix, where he shared the podium with fellow Latin-American racer Ayrton Senna a year before the latter's death in a crash into the barrier in the San Marino Grand Prix. Senna revered Fangio as his inspiration and became a triple F1 champion in emulation of Fangio, of whom he said: 'What he did in his time is something that was an example of professionalism, of courage, of style and as a man, a human being. Every year there is a winner of the championship, but not necessarily a world champion. I think Fangio is the example of a true world champion.' Fangio died two years later in 1995, at the age of 84.

2 Work with a partner.

a Texts 11A and 11B give related information from different sources. Using numbers and arrows on a copy of the texts, decide how to combine the material, without repetition of facts or ideas, so that it makes one seamless text with a logical and linked progression. First read the key point below.

Key point

Collating (combining) texts

It is a useful skill to be able to select material from two or more sources and weave it together in a way which makes a new text. This is called collation. This is how researchers use the material they find in books and on the internet. If sufficient changes to wording and structure are made to the original texts, it no longer counts as copying or plagiarism, which is not acceptable in examinations and coursework.

b Now reduce the combined text to about half its length, leaving out unnecessary detail, joining sentences together, and changing wording to make it more concise.

c Read out your final version to the class, and notice how other pairs produce different versions.

3 a Research, using a range of media, the life of someone who broke a speed record of some kind. Use more than one source of information. Make notes of the facts as a mind-map or spider diagram.

b Decide on the order in which to use your notes, and think about how to link them so that they do not sound like a list of facts.

c After reading the tip below, write a one-page biography, check it, and give it to your teacher.

For Activity 3
Writing a biography

There are various types of information which are included in a biographical outline.
- The main facts and the turning points of someone's life, with dates.
- Specific details of names and numbers, as the genre is informative.
- Examples and quotations to bring the character alive and add interest for the reader.
- A summary of what made them special and likely to be remembered, usually at the beginning or end of the piece.

Sentences should start in different ways for variety, to avoid each one beginning with *He* or *She*. The basic structure is chronological, from childhood to death or the present time, as this is the logical order in which to present someone's life story.

In this extract from a novel, a boy in New Zealand in the 1950s is riding his new bike.

Text 11C

The bike was new to me, and of course I had to pay some attention to how it went. The handlebars were stiff, but apart from that it seemed a very fine machine, and I made up my mind to really make the other kids sit up and take notice. There was no other bike at school that had a yellow frame, so that was something. Legs Hope came zooming up from behind me.

'That yours?' he said, looking at my bike. Legs had had his bike a couple of years, and his knees came right up past his handlebars as he pedalled.

'That's right,' I said. 'The very latest. My father says it is the best bike that money can buy.'

Legs rode alongside me in order to get a close look, and on the slight turn he had to make, one of his handlebars caught his knee. His bike leapt as the front wheel skidded and he flopped sideways off the seat and the next second he and his machine were bang on the road in a beautiful **gutzer**. I pulled up a few yards ahead and looked back. Legs was all tangled up in his bike. He wasn't hurt, of course. He stood up and dragged his bike with him, gave it a couple of kicks, and was back on *in a jiffy*. He rode on, and his monkey face was serious.

'I'll have to hit my old man up for a new bike,' he said. 'I'm getting too big for a boy's bike. What I need is a man's bike.'

Well, Legs was the same age as myself, and I could tell that what he said was supposed to be *a smack in the eye* for me, as his bike was the same size as mine.

'It's your legs, not the bike.'

No sooner had I said that when he swerved out to the middle of the road and the front wheel of his bike bounced into a pothole and the back wheel slid in some loose gravel. Down he went again in another beautiful gutzer. There was a clutter and yell from Legs and he turned right over on the road with the bike on top of him. He thrashed around in an awful rage, the bike wheels spinning in mid-air and his legs waving like long peasticks. I stopped again and watched him as he pulled himself out from underneath, jerked his bike up, gave it a couple more kicks, and dusted himself off. His face was red as a beetroot and he was puffing.

I didn't laugh as much as I could have, though I managed a fair amount of giggling.

'I'd like to be around when you try to ride a man's bike,' I told him.

Well, he simply squealed as he jumped on his bike. 'I'll show you, Sullivan,' he shouted. 'I'll mow you down. I'll run you down and kill you.'

I took off with a couple of metres start on him, as I saw that he was going to try to crash his bike into mine. I had to stand up on the pedals and pump my legs like a madman to keep ahead of him. Legs was *a tough customer* when he was worked up, and he wouldn't have cared if he had smashed both our bikes to **smithereens**. Over my shoulder I saw his knees absolutely jumping up and down behind his handlebars so fast they were only a bony blur, and he was leaning between them glaring at me. I really understood how he felt, his pride *having taken a knock*. Anyway, he chased me all the way to school, and rather than stop at the gates I kept right on going, steering around a bunch of kids, and on to the playground. Legs followed. The grass slowed us down, yet *our speed was still cracking* as we reached the end of the playground and I cut off to the left behind the school building and back down the other side. We must have circled the school two or three times, and though I was some distance ahead of him now, I was beginning to worry whether Legs would ever give up chasing me.

Then, passing the front of the school again I heard a loud voice I recognised, and there, on the front steps, was **Sister** Angela, with a wild face. I jammed on my brakes. Legs came around the side of the building going like fury. He saw Sister standing there and, a funny thing, he never did take his eyes off her. She looked at him and he looked right back as though he had suddenly gone off into a trance or something. He didn't finish his turn around the corner. He kept on going on, not even slowing down, till he and the bike disappeared into the hedge. The last thing I saw of him he was still goggling at Sister. Then came a tearing and wrenching, and the hedge shook for a couple of hundred metres along the roadside, as though it had been hit by a truck, and then there was complete silence. Legs had simply disappeared, that's all. Except for a few broken twigs and one or two leaves drifting around in the air, you couldn't even see where he had been. He didn't make a sound. I knew he must be just lying there in the middle of the hedge with his bike, wondering how the blazes he was going to explain it all away.

'Are you all right?' Sister Angela called out.

'Oh, yes, Sister,' said Legs from out of the hedge. 'Quite all right, thank you.'

Then she turned to me and said, 'Jimmy Sullivan, you help him out of there, tidy up the hedge after you, and the both of you will stay in after school for half an hour.'

Ian Cross, *The God Boy*

gutzer	New Zealand slang for coming a cropper, i.e. a dramatic and deserved fall
smithereens	tiny fragments
Sister	title used by nuns

4   a   Explain in more formal language the five idioms in italics in Text 11C.

b   Find and list examples of other colloquial language in the passage.

c   Explain in your own words:
   i   what makes Jimmy annoyed with Legs
   ii what makes Legs chase Jimmy.

5 **a** Plan and draw a five-box cartoon strip to represent what happens in Text 11C, using a short quotation from the passage as the caption for each box.

b List the elements of the passage that make it humorous.

Tip

For Activity 5b
Creating comedy

An incident can be made humorous, even if involving physical or mental pain for a character involved, if some of the following devices are used:

- the situation is itself inherently amusing – and a chase is a typical comedy situation and a staple of cartoons
- the actions are unrealistic in type or frequency, e.g. the number of times Legs takes a tumble. The act of falling down, whether from a cliff-top or by slipping on a banana skin, is a common one in clowning and cartoons
- one or more characters are hopelessly inept at what they are trying to do, which was the basis of Charlie Chaplin and Laurel and Hardy silent comedy films
- the appearance of one or more characters is ridiculous because of their physical characteristics or as a result of emotion, becoming angry or entranced for instance
- a character over-reacts and, for example, falls in love instantly or makes exaggerated threats, as Legs does when he says he will kill Jimmy
- the name of one or more of the characters is absurd, as is the case here
- the vocabulary choices include comic-sounding words, especially verbs, e.g. 'goggling'
- the scene contains extreme contrast, as of that between the hurtling boys and the calm nun in the school playground
- the behaviour of a character is incongruous in the context, for instance the way Legs is polite to Sister and pretends he doesn't mind having had a terrible crash
- there is an overall irony to the situation: in this case Legs thinks he deserves a man's bike because he is such a good rider.

c Think of an idea for a comic short story called 'Pride comes before a fall'. Tell the class your idea.

In Text 11D the hyphens have been deliberately removed.

Birds of a feather

The waiting room looks like any other hospital waiting room, but the patients are all wearing leather hoods and sitting on perches covered with artificial grass.

Each year, 5,000 falcons are treated at the Abu Dhabi Falcon Hospital, which is located just a few kilometres outside the city and has a staff of 65 experts. It was the first and is the largest falcon hospital, and treats falcons from all over the Emirates and the Gulf states, keeping them **in peak condition** for hunting.

The falcon is the national bird of the Emirates, and hunting with falcons is a long standing tradition in the Arab world, going back 2,000 years. Almost every Arab family has at least one falcon; the pure white females are the most sought after and **most highly prized**.

Hunting with falcons is actually banned in the UAE and nowadays they are used for sport or entered for beauty contests only, because the indigenous prey species were **being wiped out** in the region. For hunting trips the falconers go to Afghanistan, Pakistan, North Africa, China and Russia.

The Gulf's nomadic bedouin tribes used falcons to hunt, but today most birds **are bred in captivity**, and they command high prices of several thousand dollars. Their owners are devoted to them, and regard them as part of their family as well as part of their culture. They see the birds as majestic looking, fascinating and beautiful, with individual characters.

Falcons do not present symptoms of disease until they are extremely sick and it is hard for the owner to **detect an ailing bird**. The hospital therefore conducts regular check ups on falcons several times a year. They can keep up to 150 birds as in patients, and there is a boarding facility for when owners are away on business or vacation. They trim claws, polish beaks and glue back in missing feathers — necessary for flight balance — as well as treat disease.

Research on falcons is also being undertaken by the hospital, and vets and world renowned avian specialists come to study the breed. Since 2006 the hospital has treated other bird species too, everything that has wings, from canaries to ostriches.

6 **a** Six hyphens have been removed from Text 11D. On a copy of the passage, put them where they belong.

b Give synonyms for the five phrases in bold in the passage.

c Write a leaflet to promote awareness of falcons and the work of the Abu Dhabi Falcon Hospital (ADFH).

THE INCREDIBLE BIRDMAN

It took a wing, a prayer and some very special goggles to make an extraordinary flight through a mountain last week.

As he *hurtled* towards the rock face at 120 kph, Jeb Corliss suddenly realised that something was going badly wrong. He was *zooming* in from two kilometres away, flying with nothing but an aerodynamic wingsuit to hold him **aloft**, and the gap ahead through which he hoped to *swoop* looked impossibly small. It was just 30 metres wide and 12 metres high, and Corliss could see that he wasn't going to make it.

A smoke canister attached to his foot had **malfunctioned** and thrown him off his *glide* path. He was too low. Satellite navigation data being *beamed* into his high-tech goggles showed he was on course to smash into the sheer rock face below the cave entrance.

'It was horrifying', he said last week. He had only seconds to **abort** his flight by opening his parachute. 'And I knew that once I had, there wasn't going to be anywhere to land. I really thought I was going to be quite badly bashed up.' He opened the chute and spotted a small clearing in the jungle on the mountain slopes, where a landslide had *ripped* up the trees. It was hair-raisingly steep but his only hope.

For a moment last weekend it looked as if Corliss' bid to fly through the 'Gate of Heaven' in Tianmen Mountain, China, was **doomed**. But he made it down safely and was *plucked* off the mountainside by a rescue team. He was physically intact and determined to try again.

As he ascended again to 2000 metres in a helicopter, even Corliss, a **seasoned base jumper** and wingsuit flyer, struggled to control the feeling of panic. 'I have never felt such psychic pressure,' he said. 'I have never felt so scared in all my life.'

He had to hit the gap **dead-on** because, once through the 70-metre cavern, he needed to *emerge* at the right altitude to **navigate** almost over a kilometre of treacherous terrain on the other side, *swerving* around **towering** spires and *ducking* under a cable car wire before landing on a bridge three kilometres from his starting point. As for every acrobat, every movement he made would affect his chance of survival. Get it wrong

and he could crash into the forest on the far side of the cave.

As the helicopter reached the **stipulated** altitude, Corliss pulled down his helmet and goggles, spread his arms and jumped. **Clad** entirely in black, he resembled Batman. 'As I passed through the cave I remember thinking, "Wow, there are a lot of people in here watching me", and as I flew out I could see people waving and taking pictures. It was incredible: I felt like a bird.'

Sunday Times

base jumping	an extreme sport which involves jumping from high places

7 **a** Give synonyms for the ten words in bold in Text 11E.

aloft   dead-on
malfunctioned   navigate
abort   towering
doomed   stipulated
seasoned   clad

b Use the ten italicised action verbs in the passage in sentences of your own to show their meaning.

c Draw a labelled diagram of the terrain and the route of the birdman's flight, according to the information given in the passage.

8 Work with a partner.

a Find the four uses of onomatopoeia in Text 11E. What is its effect?

b What is the meaning of the following eight prefixes or word stems used in the passage? You may need to use a dictionary. Write another word you know using each of them.

mal   para   kilo   terr   psych   acro   phys   alt

c Rewrite the last four lines of the passage in indirect speech in the third person, beginning 'He said that …'.

d The word 'affect' occurs in the passage. Explain the rule for when we write *affect* and when it is spelt *effect*.

e Paraphrase in more formal language these phrases from the passage:

going to make it   badly bashed up   hair-raisingly   Get it wrong

9 a Comment on the content and effect of the second paragraph of
Text 11E.

   b Rewrite the article as a news report, selecting relevant information,
re-ordering it, and changing the style. Give it to your teacher.

   c Imagine that you were a spectator watching Corliss fly through
the Gate of Heaven. Give an account of what you witnessed and
its effect on the crowd. Read the key point below to help you.

Key point

Giving an informative account

Any recounting of an event or experience, whether descriptive,
narrative or informative, such as a witness statement, will have a
chronological structure. It will include approximate timings to show
the duration of the event and time lapses in the sequence of actions.
Measurements of distance convey the scene and the proximity and
viewpoint of the observer. The response of other witnesses is a
relevant element in an account and part of the overall impression
and record of the event.

This is the first half of a nineteenth-century gothic poem by American
writer Edgar Allan Poe.

The Raven

ONCE upon a midnight dreary, while I **pondered**, weak and weary,
Over many a quaint and curious volume of forgotten **lore**,—
While I nodded, nearly **napping**, suddenly there came a tapping,
As of some one gently rapping, rapping at my chamber door.
'Tis some visitor,' I muttered, 'tapping at my chamber door;
    Only this and nothing more.'

Ah, distinctly I remember it was in the bleak December
And each separate dying **ember wrought** its ghost upon the floor.

Eagerly I wished the morrow;—vainly I had sought to borrow
From my books **surcease** of sorrow—sorrow for the lost Lenore,
For the rare and radiant maiden whom the angels name Lenore:
   Nameless here for evermore.

And the silken sad uncertain rustling of each purple curtain
Thrilled me—filled me with fantastic terrors never felt before;
So that now, to still the beating of my heart, I stood repeating
"Tis some visitor **entreating** entrance at my chamber door,
Some late visitor entreating entrance at my chamber door:
   This it is and nothing more.'

Presently my soul grew stronger; hesitating then no longer,
'Sir,' said I, 'or Madam, truly your forgiveness I implore;
But the fact is I was napping, and so gently you came rapping,
And so faintly you came tapping, tapping at my chamber door,
That I scarce was sure I heard you'—here I opened wide the door:—
   Darkness there and nothing more.

Deep into that darkness peering, long I stood there wondering, fearing,
Doubting, dreaming dreams no mortals ever dared to dream before;
But the silence was unbroken, and the stillness gave no token,
And the only word there spoken was the whispered word, 'Lenore?'
This I whispered, and an echo murmured back the word, 'Lenore:'
   Merely this and nothing more.

Back into the chamber turning, all my soul within me burning,
Soon again I heard a tapping somewhat louder than before.
'Surely,' said I, 'surely that is something at my window lattice;
Let me see, then, what thereat is, and this mystery explore;
Let my heart be still a moment and this mystery explore:
   'Tis the wind and nothing more.'

Open here I flung the shutter, when, with many a flirt and flutter,
In there stepped a stately Raven of the saintly days of yore.
Not the least obeisance made he; not a minute stopped or stayed he;
But, with **mien** of lord or lady, perched above my chamber door,
Perched upon a **bust of Pallas** just above my chamber door:
   Perched, and sat, and nothing more.

Then this **ebony** bird **beguiling** my sad fancy into smiling
By the grave and stern decorum of the **countenance** it wore,—
'Though thy crest be shorn and shaven, thou,' I said, 'art sure no craven,

Ghastly grim and ancient Raven wandering from the Nightly shore:
Tell me what thy lordly name is on the Night's **Plutonian** shore!'
Quoth the Raven, 'Nevermore.'

mien	manner or bearing
bust of Pallas	sculpture of head and shoulders of the Greek goddess of wisdom
Plutonian	belonging to Pluto, ruler of the underworld in classical mythology

10 Discuss as a class:

a what has happened in Text 11F

b the setting and atmosphere of the poem

c what may happen later in the poem.

11 Work with a partner on Activities 11 and 12.

a Give synonyms for the ten words in bold in Text 11F.

b Comment on the language of the following five phrases from the poem:

midnight dreary   quaint and curious   rare and radiant

silken sad uncertain rustling   shorn and shaven

c What is the evidence that this is not a modern poem?

d What is the effect of the use of speech by the persona?

e What is the effect of the last word of the extract?

12 a What is the form and metre of Text 11F?

b What is the rhyme scheme of the poem?

c Write the next verse of the poem, describing what happens next:

• using the same metre and rhyme scheme

• including internal rhyme and a caesura (pause in the middle of a line) in the first and third lines

• using repetition and alliteration

• ending with the word 'more'.

Read it to the class to choose the best.

Text 11G

ATOM BOMB

In motoring, we have gone the opposite way from most inventions, which start from a practical need and gradually become safer and more stylish. Cars have become less safe and stylish, in the pursuit of speed. I present to you the Ariel Atom 300, the scariest car, ever.

Waiting for the immobiliser light to go out as you wave your keyless fob under the dash to get this crazy car going, *goosebumps* will appear in places you never thought possible. The 100 kph acceleration time of 2.9 seconds will do everything in its power to tear your clothes off you. The Ariel Atom achieves this tasty little *party trick* by not having doors. It has no roof, windscreen, rear-view mirror or body panels either, for that matter. Instead, it has an external tubular framework, a little like a crustacean shell. Yet instead of protecting the soft tissues of its occupants, the exoskeleton is wide open for a force-nine gale to howl through the framework and up your trouser leg.

I'd listened to any tidbits of advice offered by those insane enough to have already braved the 300bhp version of the Atom on the road. Firstly, they said, wear a long-sleeve top and full-length trousers and a helmet. Leave first gear alone too, I was told, so I did. Don't be too silly in second gear, either. So I wasn't. Entering my first roundabout in third gear, I planted the throttle to take my first stab at heroism, only to suddenly find myself facing in an unfamiliar direction, at a rather peculiar angle – and still accelerating.

Truth known, every time I drove the nutty, over-powered Ariel, I sighed with relief when I was parked again, in neutral, ignition off, 4-point harness unbuckled, and a metre away from the car. I'd made it back, alive.

It may take speed bumps and rough roads in its stride, but it sure doesn't look like a road car. With its skeletal construction, lacking in any sense of logic, the Atom is a loony proposition – and this one is loonier than most, fitted with an optional racing supercharger. With rear wheel drive, and engine slung out the back, the Atom bomb is somewhat rapid. *Fudge* your gear timing and you'll hit 100 kph in a *smidgen* over three seconds. A top speed of 250 kph is a finger click away, and so is the likelihood of seeing another day; the Atom is not the most stable automobile in the handling stakes, so be very wary.

Under acceleration, the Atom's front-end becomes alarmingly light and loses steering grip, which results in you and whoever was mad enough to allow you to *blag* them into the passenger seat being fired off in random directions. Definitely a little unsafe; but then again, you might as well go out with a bang.

Etihad Inflight Magazine

13 **a** What do the following five colloquialisms used in italics in Text 11G mean?

goosebumps   party trick   fudge   smidgen   blag

b Use the following expressions from the passage in sentences of your own to show their meaning:

to take a stab at   to take something in one's stride   to go out with a bang

c The adjectives 'insane', 'mad', 'crazy', 'silly', 'nutty' and 'loony' are all used in the passage. Rank order them according to increasing strength of meaning.

14 Work with a partner.

a Look at the following punctuation and syntactical devices used in Text 11G and comment on their effect:
   i the last comma in the first paragraph; the dash at the end of the third paragraph; the last comma in the fourth paragraph
   ii the sentence beginning 'It has no roof…' in the second paragraph.

b Look at the following stylistic devices used in the passage and comment on their effect:
   i Truth known   Fudge your gear timing   Definitely a little unsafe
   ii somewhat rapid   not the most stable automobile   a little unsafe

c Do you think the writer is recommending that the reader should experience driving the Ariel Atom 300? Summarise the reason for your answer.

15 Imagine you have been asked to test drive and review a new vehicle. Research some facts, add ideas of your own if you wish, and then write your review, using the tone and style of Text 11G.

For Activity 15
Writing a product review

Like any other review, a report on something which has been tested or taken on a trial run will contain an evaluation. Reviews are often made more engaging by the use of idioms and colloquial language, dramatic expressions, and even humour. The subject pronoun *You* is used to include the reader in the experience. The pace is brisk, contributed to by the use of elliptical (shortened) forms of common phrases, e.g. 'Truth known', for 'If the truth be known'.

This is the imaginary blog account of Ottone Baggio, the Italian designer of the Aerogallo (Flying Rooster).

File   Edit   View   History   Bookmarks   Help

I was enjoying an evening with some friends when one of them challenged me to design a plane in the shape of a cockerel. So I took a napkin and sketched it out on the spot. Why not?

It was a completely mad idea, which is why I liked it! Roosters rarely fly, so no one could say mine was not lifelike! Most people, when they design an aeroplane, think about boring things like aerodynamics. For me, the paint scheme was much more important. And, of course, it had to look like a rooster. If it could fly safely despite the shape, so much the better. In order to get the rooster's head, I had to make the engine stick up and out at the end of a nice curved neck ... no one has ever made such a ridiculous design for a plane, I think. But how the *bambini* love it! They expect it to make cock-a-doodle-doo noises – so it does! I have a loudspeaker built into its talons – well, wheels – and I have a DVD player in the cockpit – what an appropriate name! – with 15 different kinds of cockerel calls to blast out as I go.

Although I did my best to make the shape of the plane look like a male chicken, in truth it was nothing like the bird until my brilliant friend Giuliano Basso took over

the painting. He was inspired by a little-known painting of two cockerels by the Italian naive artist Antonio Ligabue. The feathers in that painting are of such fabulous colours and texture – that's how he brought my wonderful Aerogallo to life. Look at it! It's a unique work of art, and the children laugh. That's what it's all about, making children laugh.

All the serious pilots who saw it laughed at my magnificent plane, and refused absolutely to go up in it. Fortunately, I then met Daniele Beltrame, an intrepid airman who has much more imagination than sense! He agreed to take my Aerogallo into the air for its maiden flight. So, finally, on 26 December 2011, at the tiny airfield of Nervesa in my native Italy, the Aerogallo 'flapped its wings' and took to the sky. It flew like a bird! I take it to all the airshows in Italy, and now it's also famous all over the world, thanks to the internet, and people beg me to bring it to their displays, so their children can see the 'Flying Rooster', and the madman who designed it.

You can see the whole story of the birth of the Aerogallo at
http://issuu.com/dashound/docs/aerogallo_story_final_versionsing

 a Read Text 11H and explain in your own words of one sentence each:
 i why Ottone Baggio wanted to design and build such an unusual plane
 ii what difficulties he had to overcome
 iii what he enjoys about it.

b How does the blog show the writer's enthusiasm for his plane?

c What makes the blog sound like spoken language?

d Write a news report for the Flying Rooster's first flight. Give it your own headline. Use as much information from the text as you can but choose a different sequence, style, voice and time perspective. Include some direct speech.

e Swap your report with a partner to check accuracy, then correct it and give it to your teacher.

UNIT 12 Seeing things differently

This unit includes a look at facts versus opinions, bias, empathy, prediction, and the collating and sequencing of material. There is practice of sentence structures, transitional adverbials, prefixes, hyphens, dashes, summary, and more phrasal verbs. The tasks are to script a news interview; take part in group discussion; write a news article and an encyclopaedia entry; evaluate an argument; research and write a formal report.

Activities

1

a Make a mind-map of ways in which scientific discoveries and inventions have affected your daily life.

b What do you think science will make possible in the future?

c What do you wish science had never made possible?

Text 12A

The miracle razor blade sharpener

Many people believe and have tried to prove that the Great Pyramid at Giza in Egypt, known as the Cheops or Khufu pyramid, has paranormal **properties** because of its shape. In particular, they believe that it has the ability to preserve food and to sharpen razor blades. Here is the process to be followed: cut four equilateral triangles of any size from cardboard; construct a pyramid by taping the sides of the triangle sides together; align the pyramid so that the baselines point at magnetic north and south.

The French hardware-store owner Antoine Bovis claimed in 1930 that small models of pyramids have restorative and preservative properties. **Unverifiable** stories persist that Bovis discovered this paranormal force whilst inside the King's Chamber of the Great

Pyramid. According to legend, he noticed that animals that had wandered into the pyramid and died there had not decomposed, and he deduced that it was the shape of the pyramid which was preventing their decay. Bovis is on record as having denied ever visiting Egypt. He claims that he arrived at his pseudoscientific belief through a process of reason and experiment. He explains in his self-published book that he built a model of the pyramid and proved to his own satisfaction that pieces of meat and fish became **mummified**.

Inspired by Bovis, a Czech called Drbal applied for a **patent** for the 'Pharaoh's Shaving Device', which allegedly used the magnetic field generated by cardboard model pyramids to keep razor blades sharp. He was not able to explain how exactly it worked. Investigation revealed that similar claims had been made about 'pyramid power' decades earlier.

In 2005, in an episode of *MythBusters* on the television Discovery Channel, a basic test of pyramid power was performed, using pyramids built to the specifications found in pyramid-power claims. Food, a flower and then a razor blade were placed in the pyramid, and a control test was also **conducted** for the three items. There was no **appreciable** difference between the state of the items within and without the pyramid. Some people believe that the paranormal cannot be disproved and did not accept that the myth had been proved to be false.

patent	licence for the exclusive right to produce an invention

2 a Explain in your own words the following words as used in bold in Text 12A:

properties   unverifiable   mummified   conducted   appreciable

b Look at the following prefixes or word stems and state their meanings as used in the passage. Write another word you know using each of them.

para   equi   pseudo   gen   spec

c Find places in the passage where it would be logical to insert one of the following discourse markers at the beginning of a sentence:

Moreover,   In addition,

Furthermore,   However,

Nevertheless,

3 **a** Copy and complete the table below with the facts and opinions in Text 12A. Add more rows if you need them.

fact	opinion

b What is your view on the subject of pyramid power, based on the passage, and why?

c Which words and phrases in the passage show the bias (own opinion) of the writer on the subject?

Text 12B is from the famous gothic horror novel, *Frankenstein* by Mary Shelley. The scientist is horrified by what he has done in creating a monster. Henry Clerval is Doctor Frankenstein's close friend.

Doctor Frankenstein's voice

I trembled excessively; I could not **endure** to think of, and far less to **allude** to, the occurrences of the **preceding** night. I walked with a quick pace, and we soon arrived at my college. I then reflected, and the thought made me shiver, that the creature whom I had left in my apartment might still be there, alive, and walking about. I dreaded to behold this monster; but I feared still more that Henry should see him. **Entreating** him, therefore, to remain a few minutes at the bottom of the stairs, I darted up towards my own room. My hand was already on the lock of the door before I **recollected** myself. I then paused; and a cold shivering came over me. I threw the door forcibly open, as children are accustomed to do when they expect a spectre to stand in waiting for them on the other side; but nothing appeared. I stepped fearfully in: the apartment was empty; and my bedroom was also freed from its **hideous** guest. I could hardly believe that so great a good fortune could have **befallen** me; but when I became **assured** that my enemy had indeed fled, I clapped my hands for joy, and ran down to Clerval.

We ascended into my room, and the servant **presently** brought breakfast; but I was unable to contain myself. It was not joy only that possessed me; I felt my flesh tingle with excess of sensitiveness, and my pulse beat rapidly. I was unable to remain for a single instant in the same place; I jumped over the chairs, clapped my hands, and laughed aloud. Clerval at first **attributed** my unusual spirits to joy on his arrival; but when he observed me more attentively he saw a wildness in my eyes for which he could not account; and my loud, unrestrained, heartless laughter frightened and astonished him.

Work in a small group on Activities 4 and 5.

 a Replace the ten words in bold in Text 12B with synonyms.

endure	allude
preceding	entreating
recollected	hideous
befallen	assured
presently	attributed

b How has physical behaviour been used to create mood?

c What makes the reader empathise with Dr Frankenstein in this extract?

The nameless monster has left the town of Geneva and gone to hide in the countryside, where he sleeps in the barn of a poor brother and sister who live with their elderly and blind father.

Frankenstein's Monster's voice

I lay on my straw, but I could not sleep. I thought of the occurrences of the day. What chiefly struck me was the gentle manners of these people; and I longed to join them, but dared not. I remembered too well the treatment I had suffered the night before from the barbarous villagers, and resolved, whatever course of conduct I might hereafter think it right to pursue, that for the present I would remain quietly in my hovel, watching, and endeavouring to discover the motives which influenced their actions.

The cottagers arose the next morning before the sun. The young woman arranged the cottage, and prepared the food; and the youth departed after the first meal.

This day was passed in the same routine as that which preceded it. The young man was constantly employed out of doors, and the girl in various laborious occupations within. The old man, whom I soon perceived to be blind, employed his leisure hours on his instrument or in contemplation. Nothing could exceed the love and respect which the younger cottagers exhibited towards their venerable companion. They performed towards him every little office of affection and duty with gentleness; and he rewarded them by his benevolent smiles.

They were not entirely happy. The young man and his companion often went apart, and appeared to weep. I saw no cause for their unhappiness; but I was deeply affected by it. If such lovely creatures were miserable, it was less strange that I, an imperfect and solitary being, should be wretched. Yet why were these gentle beings unhappy? They possessed a delightful house (for such it was in my eyes) and every luxury; they had a fire to warm them when chill, and delicious viands when hungry; they were dressed in excellent clothes; and, still more, they enjoyed one another's company and speech, interchanging each day looks of affection and kindness.

By degrees I made a discovery of still greater moment. I found that these people possessed a method of communicating their experience and feelings to one another by articulate sounds. I perceived that the words they spoke sometimes produced pleasure or pain, smiles or sadness, in the minds and countenances of the hearers. This was indeed a godlike science, and I ardently desired to become acquainted with it. By great application, however, and after having remained during the space of several revolutions of the moon in my hovel, I discovered the names that were given to some of the most familiar objects of discourse; I learned and applied the words, *fire, milk, bread,* and *wood.* I learned also the names of the cottagers themselves. The youth and his companion had each of them several names, but the old man had only one, which was *father.* The girl was called *sister,* or *Agatha*; and the youth *Felix, brother,* or *son.* I cannot describe the delight I felt when I learned the ideas appropriated to each of these sounds, and was able to pronounce them.

Mary Shelley

5 a Quote the words and phrases from Text 12C which create pathos (sympathy based on pity) for the monster.

b Put into your own words this sentence from the passage:

By great application, however, and after having remained during the space of several revolutions of the moon in my hovel, I discovered the names that were given to some of the most familiar objects of discourse;

c Summarise in one sentence each what the monster is saying in the passage about:
   i himself
   ii the people
   iii their language.

d Discuss in your group whether you think the scientist or the monster deserves more sympathy for the situation they now both find themselves in, referring to the passages to support your views.

e Basing your response on inference from the two passages, discuss what you think is likely to happen next and how the story might end.

In Text 12D on the next page the physicist Dr Brian Cox talks about his job designing the world's largest particle accelerator at the Nuclear Research Centre (Cern) in Geneva.

Text 12D

EXPLORING THE UNIVERSE

I'm terrible at waking up – I hate it. If I can get away with it, I get up at 9 o'clock. I stay in a little Holiday Inn, close to Cern at the foothills of the Jura mountains in France. They knock on the door with breakfast so I <u>am made</u> to get up. I get the *Herald Tribune* delivered and *pain au chocolat* and coffee.

Cern is one big physics lab a 20-minute walk away, across the border into Switzerland. You can see Mont Blanc – it's absolutely beautiful and **it makes my day**.

I've always been a scientist, always. From as far back as I can remember I wanted <u>to do</u> something about space exploration or astronomy. I didn't go to university until I was 22. Instead I joined a rock band called 'Dare'. We <u>made</u> two albums and toured for a few years. Then we split up, so I rang Manchester University and said, 'Right, I want to come to uni now and <u>do physics</u>.'

It's an odd job – a fantastic job actually. Your job description is 'Find out **what makes the universe tick**, and here's this €6 billion machine that you can use <u>to do it</u>.' The aim of the project is to find the origin of mass in the universe. That really means: 'Why is this table solid?' Everything indicates that when the universe began, everything was exactly like light, and it had no mass. As it expanded and cooled, something happened to cause things to get heavy. We know exactly where in time that happened, but we don't know exactly what it was that happened. The machine's been built specifically to go to that place and watch that process unfold.

Lunch is at 12, and the canteen is packed with thousands of physicists, all mingling and talking about physics. <u>What we're doing</u> here really is as exciting as it sounds. It's exploration, just like going to the moon or Mars, or looking over the horizon to somewhere you've never seen before.

The particle accelerator we're building is a massive ring with a 27-kilometre circumference, buried about 100 metres underground. It's cold inside that tube, minus 271°C, colder than space. We send proton beams around in both directions and smash them together up to 600m times a second.

In that moment of collision – less than a billionth of a second – you get extreme conditions, like the very early universe. The area of the machine that's closest to the collisions is in an immense cavern, like a giant camera, and it takes pictures, so you can see what's happened. Someone once said it's like getting two Swiss watches and smashing them together, and then looking at the bits and **trying to make out** what was inside and how it works.

The trick with this kind of project is to think outside the box. It's really up to you **what you make of it**. At the moment our knowledge stops at really simple but profound places, like: 'Why is gravity such a weak force? The whole planet is pulling this glass down, yet I can just pick it up.' That's a huge mystery, and understanding **it would make for** a complete reassessment of how the universe works.

At around 7 everyone goes out for a meal, perhaps in the village. I usually chat on the computer to my family when I get back. I can't fall asleep without reading. It <u>doesn't do</u> for it to be physics though, or I wouldn't go to sleep.

Sunday Times Magazine

Work with a partner on Activities 6 and 7.

6 a Look at the following five prefixes or word stems used in Text 12D and state their meanings. Give another word using each of them.

astro   uni   circum   grav   proto

b Rephrase these five colloquialisms in more formal language:

I'm terrible at   get away with it   split up

packed with   think outside the box

c Look at the underlined uses of various forms of the verbs *do* and *make* in the passage. Try to formulate a rule for the difference between the two verbs.

d Explain the following five phrases in bold in the passage using your own words:

it makes my day   what makes the universe tick

trying to make out   what you make of it   it would make for

e List as many phrasal verbs using *do* and *make* as you can think of, in two columns. Compare your lists with those of other pairs.

For Activities 6c and 6e
Do and *make*

These verbs are two of the most frequently used verbs in English, and a wide range of phrasal verbs can be formed from them, only a few of which are included in the passage. There is a tendency by students to get them confused, and to say things like 'I did a mistake'. Generally speaking, in their primary form *do* is more likely to refer to an action, and *make* is more often used for the creation of something. You need to be aware that these phrasal verbs have many idiomatic usages.

7 a What strikes you as interesting or surprising about Dr Brian Cox in Text 12D?

b Collect a list of facts from the passage about his character and beliefs.

c Write and perform the script of a news programme interview with Dr Brian Cox, set out as a Q and A dialogue. Use the passage as the basis for the questions.

Text 12E

File   Edit   View   History   Bookmarks   Help

May 2012

Felix Baumgartner, otherwise known as Fearless Felix, the 43-year-old Austrian base jumper and daredevil, is about to jump from a helium balloon 39 kilometres above a remote part of New Mexico. If he succeeds, he will become the first man to go supersonic without the help of an aeroplane. At this altitude the atmosphere is very thin and air pressure hardly exists. It is almost a vacuum, and as a result Baumgartner will be unable to correct a spin using wind resistance in the way a skydiver can at less extreme altitudes. The only way he has been able to practise is with bungee-jumps. *If he survives, he will break three records in addition to becoming the first supersonic man: the highest altitude reached in a balloon, the highest skydive, and the longest freefall. Even if his state-of-the-art pressurised suit functions and his legs stay symmetrical as he breaks the sound barrier, his concerns are far from over: his parachute might freeze; his balloon might explode; his oxygen supply might run out.*

When asked why anyone would want to perform such a daring feat, Baumgartner says that records are made to be broken, and that he needed a new challenge, having jumped from all of the highest buildings in the world. He also explains that the scientific purpose of the mission is to find out whether ultra-high-altitude bail-outs from spacecraft are possible. If the space shuttle Columbia had held together for 20 seconds more when it malfunctioned in 2003, it would have been at an altitude where it would have been survivable to eject. He denies being an adrenaline junkie, but admits to having wanted to become a real-life Batman since a small child, when he was always climbing trees and towers. After the balloon jump, the ex-military man – he spent five years in the Austrian army parachute display team – intends to become a fire-fighting helicopter pilot, spending half the year in the USA and half in Austria doing mountain rescue.

October 2012

On the 14th of this month the 43-year-old Austrian daredevil leapt from a helium balloon 39 kilometres above the earth and into the world-record books for the first person to break the sound barrier and for the highest manned balloon flight. He reached 1357 kph and his ten-minute jump was watched by more than 8 million people on YouTube – another record, for a live news event on the website. He had to wait 12 days for the right weather conditions. He said he almost aborted his jump because his helmet visor steamed up. He was in free-fall for four minutes 20 seconds before deploying his parachute. He started by tumbling head-over-heels instead of adopting the necessary delta position with arms swept back.

8 **a** Comment on the construction of the italicised part of Text 12E.

b Before checking in the passage, copy the following phrases and put hyphens in the correct places:

43 year old Austrian base jumper
his state of the art pressurised suit
ultra high altitude bail outs
fire fighting helicopter pilot
the world record books

c Rewrite the following sentences from the passage to include one or more dashes.
  i Felix Baumgartner otherwise known as Fearless Felix is about to jump from a hot-air balloon.
  ii If he survives he will break three records in addition to becoming the first supersonic man.
  iii On the 14th of this month the Austrian daredevil leapt from a helium balloon 39 kilometres above the earth and set a record for the first person to break the sound barrier.

d Rewrite the last four sentences of the passage as one sentence.

e Rewrite the sentences below using a subordinating connective. You may need to change the order of the clauses.
  i It is almost a vacuum, and as a result Baumgartner will be unable to correct a spin using wind resistance in the way a skydiver can at less extreme altitudes.
  ii Baumgartner says that records are made to be broken, and that he needed a new challenge, having jumped from all of the highest buildings in the world.
  iii He denies being an adrenaline junkie, but admits to having wanted to become a real-life Batman.

9 Now you are going to use Text 12E for three different purposes, using different information and styles. Write one paragraph for each, having planned your answers first.

a Write Felix Baumgartner's journal entry for May 2012.

b Write a news bulletin of Felix Baumgartner's achievement on 14 October 2012.

c Write an entry on Felix Baumgartner for an online encyclopaedia.

10 Work in a group.

   a Think about your views on base jumping and the kind of extreme feats performed by Felix Baumgartner and others you have read about in this book.

   b Plan some things to say about whether such pursuits should be encouraged, or whether they are unnatural and unnecessary.

   c Take part in a group discussion activity, which your teacher will observe and evaluate as a speaking and listening task.

11 Evaluate the argument presented in Text 12F. Write a page in response to the case being presented in the article, saying where and why you do or do not agree with the claims of the writer. You may include your own knowledge and ideas when engaging with those in the passage.

Key point

Evaluating an argument

It is an important skill to learn not only how to present a convincing argument yourself – needed in both language and literature studies – but how to assess and judge someone else's attempt to convince you of something. The way to do this is to identify the claims being made, and then assess their validity by examining the way they have been presented. You do not need to know anything about a topic to be able to evaluate the validity of an argument. There are various ways in which writers attempt to manipulate readers and their opinions, and you need to recognise these. They are:

- using statistics to sound impressive, but in fact they may not be relevant or significant
- referring to famous names and alleging that they support the view of the writer; even if this is the case, it does not mean that the view being expressed is a valid one
- repetition of ideas, slightly rephrased, to make there seem to be more arguments than there really are
- exaggerated claims which are patently untrue
- using dramatic and sensational language for emotive effect
- vagueness about who has provided the evidence or made a statement
- mockery of the other point of view
- making no mention that there is another point of view
- using 'we' to try to include the reader in the writer's point of view.

Have humans really stood on the moon?

One of the most well known of all conspiracy theories – along with those concerning the assassination of U.S. President J.F. Kennedy, the death of British Princess Diana, and 9/11 – is whether there was ever a moon landing by Apollo astronauts in June 1969. As it has continued for forty years, there must be some truth behind the belief that the moon landing was a hoax staged by NASA (National Aeronautics and Space Administration) in order to win the space race going on at the time between the USA and Russia. The claims are that evidence was manufactured, destroyed or tampered with, and that this included photos, tape recordings, rock samples, and the testimony of witnesses. The general thesis is that the landing was filmed in a studio with painted scenery and fake props.

One conspiracist examined microscopically the photo of the astronauts emerging from the landing craft and said he can pinpoint where a spotlight was used to simulate sunlight, and calculated that it was between 24 and 36 centimetres to the right of the camera. It has also been cited as evidence for it being a hoax that no stars are visible though they should have been, that the background to all of the photographs is the same, and that the flag fluttered, as if in a fan breeze, despite there being no wind on the moon.

There have been detailed rebuttals of the hoax allegations, but polls taken in various places have shown that between 6% and 20% even of Americans believe that the manned landings between 1969 and 1972 were faked, and major USA television networks have broadcast documentaries about the conspiracy theory. The rebuttal is founded upon the alleged existence of photos taken of the Apollo landing site showing the tracks left by the astronauts, and of the Apollo-planted stars and stripes flag still standing on the moon. But we all know that photographs can be doctored and that they prove nothing. An episode of *MythBusters* in August 2008 tested many of the conspiracists' claims and labelled them as being 'busted', meaning that they had been found to be untrue. But then they would, wouldn't they, since that is the purpose of the programme.

12 You are going to write a formal report to give to your teacher for assessment. Use the key point below to help you.

  a Choose a scientific topic referred to in any of the texts in this unit, or which is an interest of your own, to do some further research on.

  b Collect notes from the sources you use for your research online or in printed materials.

  c Organise your notes into a logical structure.

  d Write your report in sentences and paragraphs.

  e Check your piece carefully before you give it to your teacher.

Key point

Formal report

A formal report is a clearly structured piece of writing expressed in formal language which has an informative or evaluative aim. Reports are typically written after research or an investigation has been carried out. The material needs to be relevant and sequenced, and often arrives at a recommendation or conclusion. The personal feelings of the writer are not relevant and the perspective taken must be a purely objective one. The content is factual and draws on evidence. The tone is dispassionate (without emotion or any indication of the personality of the writer) and the style is plain and clear, using mature and precise vocabulary similar to that of scientific writing.

Acknowledgements

The authors and publishers acknowledge the following sources of copyright material and are grateful for the permissions granted. While every effort has been made, it has not always been possible to identify the sources of all the material used, or to trace all copyright holders. If any omissions are brought to our notice, we will be happy to include the appropriate acknowledgements on reprinting.

p. 5 adapted from 'The puzzle of the giant pictures' by Hester Davenport for The Early Times, published in The Early Times Book of Unsolved Mysteries, used with permission; p. 12 'Maggie and Milly and Molly and May' by EE Cummings, used by permission of WW Norton Publishing; p. 15 adapted from article 'Pacific Rubbish Dump twice the size…' by Anna Davies © The Evening Standard, published 5 February 2008; p. 25 'The Planners' from Another Place by Kim Cheng Boey, by permission of the author; p. 27 'Living off other people – Welfare' by Jenny Joseph, copyright © Jenny Joseph, SELECTED POEMS, Bloodaxe 1992. Reproduced with permission of Johnson & Alcock Ltd; p. 30 adapted from article 'OMG Cupid – this is the written word's golden age' by Mark Forsyth in the Sunday Times, October 2012, NewsSyndication.com; p. 32 adapted from article 'Language is forever changing, innit?' by Adrian Mourby in the TES, July 2001; p. 34 adapted from AFP article 'Languages dying out at rapid pace', reported in the Bangkok Post, October 2007; p. 36 adapted from article 'They're kids just like me, only hungry' by Martha Payne in the Sunday Times, October 2012, NewsSyndication.com; p. 37 adapted from article 'Nice chatting to you, Jonah' by Francesca Angelini in the Sunday Times, October 2012, NewsSyndication.com; p. 42 excerpt from ZLATA'S DIARY: A CHILD'S LIFE IN SARAJEVO by Zlata Filipovic, translated by Christina Pribichevich-Zoric, translation © 1994 by Fixot et Editions Robert Laffont. Used by permission of Viking Penguin, a division of Penguin Group (USA) LLC; p. 43 'Nigeria we hail thee' by Lillian Jean Williams, 1960, the national anthem of Nigeria; p. 47 'Geography Lesson' by Zulfikar Ghose. Copyright © Zulfikar Ghose 1967, reproduced by permission of Zulfikar Ghose; p. 48 'Gift for the Darkness' from LORD OF THE FLIES by William Golding, copyright 1954, renewed © 1982 by William Gerald Golding. Used by permission of G.P. Putnam's Sons, a division of Penguin Group (USA) LLC, and by permission of Faber and Faber Ltd as publisher; p. 51 'Nothing's Changed' by Tatamkhulu Afrika; p. 62 NINETEEN EIGHTY FOUR by George Orwell (copyright © George Orwell, 1949) by permission of Bill Hamilton as the Literary Executor of the Estate of the late Sonia Brownell Orwell. Adapted with permission. Copyright 1949 by Houghton Mifflin Harcourt Publishing Company. Copyright © renewed 1977 by Sonia Brownell Orwell. Reprinted by permission of Houghton Mifflin Publishing Company. All rights reserved; p. 64 excerpt from 'The Pedestrian' by Ray Bradbury. Reprinted by permission of Don Congdon Associates, Inc. © 1951 by the Fortnightly Publishing Company, renewed 1979 by Ray Bradbury; p. 66 'The Prisoner' by Susan Howe published in Triclops, © Susan Howe, used by permission of the author; p. 69 adapted from article 'Technology in the home of the future' by Matt Warman in the Telegraph, 8 October 2012 © Telegraph Media Group Limited 2012; p. 71 from Letters to Daniel copyright © Fergal Keane 1996. Reproduced by permission of the author c/o Rogers, Coleridge & White Ltd, 20 Powis Mews London W11 1JN; p. 75 'The Road Not Taken' by Robert Frost from The Poetry of Robert Frost edited by Edward Connery Latham, published by Jonathan Cape, reprinted by permission of The Random House Group Limited. Copyright © 1916, 1969 by Henry Holt and Company, copyright © 1944 by Robert Frost. Reprinted by permission of Henry Holt and Company LLC. Users are warned that this Selection is protected under copyright laws and downloading is strictly prohibited. The right to reproduce or transfer this Selection via any medium must be secured from Henry Holt and Company LLC; p. 82 'Choices' by Robert Stone; p. 85 'The Three Princes' retold by Elaine L. Lindy from www.storiesgrowby.com; pp. 91 and 93 adapted from articles by Ruchina Hoon and Neha Bhayana in the Hindustan Times, September 2009; p. 94 adapted from article 'More than words' by Queen Rania of Jordan in the Sunday Times, April 2009, NewsSyndication.com; p. 96 adapted from article 'Touchy-feel robot to teach in schools' by Liz Lightfoot in the Sunday Times, February 2013, NewsSyndication.com; p. 97 'Head of English' by Carol Ann Duffy is taken from Standing Female Nude by Carol Ann Duffy published by Anvil Press Poetry in 1985; p. 99 'Flying into the Wind' is the second of a quartet of films written by David Leland under the generic title 'Tales out of School'. Used by permission of the author; p. 104 adapted from article 'Have a helping of shame. It will stop you wasting food' by Minette Marrin in the Sunday Times, January 2013, NewsSyndication.com; p. 106 adapted from article 'Restored ring rescues homeless guy' by Will Pavia published in The Australian and The Times, March 2013, NewsSyndication.com; p. 107 from 'The Ultimate Safari' from Jump by Nadine Gordimer, from the collected work Life Times: Stories 1952–2007, by permission of AP Watt at United Agents on behalf of Felix Licensing BV. Reprinted by permission of Russell & Volkening as agent for the author, copyright © 1991 by Felix Licensing BV. Reprinted by permission of Penguin Books Canada Inc. Reprinted by permission of Farrar, Straus and Giroux, LLC; p. 111 from THE DIARY OF A YOUNG GIRL: THE DEFINITIVE EDITION by Anne Frank, edited by Otto H Frank and Mirjam Pressler, translated by Susan Massotty (Viking, 1997) copyright © The Anne Frank-Fonds, Basle, Switzerland, 1991. English translation © Doubleday, a division of Bantam Doubleday Dell Publishing Group Inc, 1995. Reproduced by permission of Penguin Books Ltd. Used by permission of Doubleday, an imprint of the Knopf Doubleday Publishing Group, a division of Random House LLC. All rights reserved (any third party use of this material, outside of this publication, is prohibited. Interested parties must apply directly to Random House LLC for permission); p. 114 letter based on an appeal by the World Wildlife Fund; p. 116 text from the tiger fact file on www.arkive.org, used by permission of Wildscreen; p. 118 excerpt from Practical Ways to Crack Crime: The Handbook published by the Home Office, 1989; p. 120 from The No. 1 Ladies' Detective Agency by Alexander McCall Smith, published by Birlinn Limited; p. 124 adapted from article 'Caped doggy doo-gooder takes Czech law enforcement into his own hands' by Bojan Pancevski in the Sunday Times, October 2011, NewsSyndication.com; p. 125 abridged excerpt from 'The Destructors' by Graeme Greene, used with adaptations by permission of David Higham Associates; p. 129 excerpt from 'A Hero' from Under the Banyan Tree by R.K. Narayan, published by Random House; p. 133 'Visitors' from Studying Literature by Brian Moon. Copyright © 1989 by Chalkface Press Pty Ltd. Reprinted by permission of Chalkface Press and Brian Moon; p. 138 adapted from article 'It's sweltering out here, mate' (A life in the day) interview by Simon Crerar in the Sunday Times Magazine, January 2013, NewsSyndication.com; p. 141 from THE VILLAGE BY THE SEA by Anita Desai (Penguin Books 1984, 1988, 1992, 2001). Copyright © Anita Desai, 1982. Reproduced by permission of Penguin Books Ltd, and reproduced by permission of the author c/o Rogers, Coleridge & White Ltd., 20 Powis Mews, London W11 1JN; p. 147 'Bukit Timah, Simgapore' by Lee Tzu Pheng, by permission of the author; p. 149 adapted from article 'Master Kishan: world's youngest director' (A life in the day) interview by Beverley D'Silva in Sunday Times Magazine, March 2008, NewsSyndication.com; p. 151 'Carpet-weavers, Morocco' by Carol Rumens; p. 152 'Monologue' by Hone Tuwhare, first published in No Ordinary Sun, 1964, also published in Small Holes in the Silence: Collected Works,

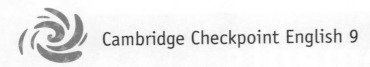

Godwit Press, Random House NZ, 2011. © Rob Tuwhare on behalf of the Estate of Hone Tuwhare, honetuwharepoetry@gmail.com; p. 158 from *The God Boy* by Ian Cross, © 1957, used by permission from Penguin New Zealand; p. 163 adapted from article 'The incredible birdman' by Rosie Kinchen in the Sunday Times, October 2011, NewsSyndication.com; p. 168 adapted from article 'Atom Bomb' by Jon Saxon in Etihad in-flight magazine, November 2007; p. 178 adapted from 'Dr Brian Cox, exploring the universe' (A life in the day) interview by Charlotte Hunt-Grubbe in the Sunday Times Magazine, August 2008, NewsSyndication.com

Thanks to the following for permission to reproduce copyright photographs:

Cover Thor Jorgen Udvang/Shutterstock; p. 1 Mediacolor's/Alamy; p. 3 RGB Ventures LLC dba SuperStock/Alamy; p. 5 iStock/Thinkstock; p. 7 Free Art License 1.3/J.-N. L; p. 10 With kind permission of Blek le Rat; p. 12 Marylooo/Thinkstock; p. 13 (money) iStock/Boboling/Thinkstock, (flat pack furniture) iStock/Thinkstock, (velcro) Hemera/Thinkstock, (barcode) Shutterstock.com/Claudio Divizia, (bicycle) The Keasbury-Gordon Photograph Archive/Alamy; p. 14 Mtoome/Thinkstock; p. 15 Shutterstock.com/Ulrich Mueller; p. 16 Shutterstock.com/Luiz Rocha; p. 20 Shutterstock.com/Igor Zakowski; p. 23 Shutterstock.com/Sam72; p. 26 Shutterstock.com/joyfull; p. 27 iStock/Thinkstock; p. 29 Olga Serdyuk/iStock/Thinkstock; p. 30 Ryan Putnam/iStock/Thinkstock; p. 32 Ronnie McMillan/Alamy; p. 34 Ludo Kuipers/Corbis; p. 36 Mary's Meals; p. 37 Shutterstock.com/Miles Away Photography; p. 39 Macrovector/Thinkstock/iStock; p. 41 Thinkstock/Fuse; p. 43 Thinkstock/iStock; p. 46 Shutterstock.com/Igor Zakowski; p. 47 Shutterstock.com/Brian Kinney; p. 48 Pictorial Press Ltd/Alamy; p. 51 Otofreaks/Thinkstock/iStock; p. 55 PARAMOUNT/THE KOBAL COLLECTION; p. 59 SONY PICTURES ENTERTAINMENT/THE KOBAL COLLECTION; p. 62 COLUMBIA/THE KOBAL COLLECTION; p. 63 Thinkstock/Saurabh Mehandru; p. 64 DieKleinert/Alamy; p. 66 Shutterstock.com/Mopic; p. 69 Fanatic Studio/Alamy; p. 71 Thinkstock/Igor Dmitriev; p. 72 Shutterstock.com/Songquan Den; p. 74 iStock/Thinkstock/Stacey Newman; p. 75 Shutterstock.com/Costall; p. 77 Mike Baldwin/Cornered/CartoonStock; p. 80 iStock/Thinkstock/Koosen; p. 81 REX/Ray Tang; p. 82 Shutterstock.com/Sunsinger; p. 84 (water droplet) Thinkstock /iStock /Giovanni Banfi, (waterfall and bottle) Thinkstock/laurent Renault; p. 85 Shutterstock.com/Rudolf Tepfenhart; p. 87 Thinkstock/Spike Mafford; p. 90 Thinkstock/Martin Poole; p. 91 Daniel Heighton/Alamy; p. 93 Thinkstock/iStock/Cifotart; p. 94 Shutterstock.com/Monkey Business Images; p. 96 The Sunday Times/NewsSyndication.com; p. 97 Mary Evans Picture Library/S.B. DAVIE; p. 99 Thinkstock/Moodboard; p. 102 Danita Delimont/Alamy; p. 103 Shutterstock.com/Dmitrijs Bindemanis; p. 104 Aaron Ansarov/Getty Images; p. 106 James Breeden/Splash News/Corbis; p. 108 G Friedrich Stark/Alamy; p. 110 Peter Turnley/CORBIS; p. 111 Keystone Pictures USA/Alamy; p. 114 iStock/Andyworks; p. 115 Shutterstock.com/neelsky; p. 118 Andrew Butterton/Alamy; p. 120 Thinkstock/iStock; p. 122 REX/c.HBO/Everett; p. 126 Thinkstock/iStock; p. 129 Valerie Armstrong/Alamy; p. 131 Thinkstock/Getty Images; p. 133 Shutterstock.com/Rob Wilson; p. 136 Thinkstock/iStock/Melinda Fawver; p. 138 Shutterstock.com/Tomas1111; p. 141 Shutterstock.com/Santhosh Kumar; p. 142 Thinkstock/Uros Ravbar; p. 144 Shutterstock.com/iurii; p. 147 Shutterstock.com/JPL Designs; p. 149 Ami Vitale/Getty Images; p. 151 Shutterstock.com/Vladimir Melnik; p. 153 Thinkstock/iStock/Levent Konuk; p. 155 The Print Collector/Alamy; p. 156 Getty Images for Shell; p. 158 Mary Evans/Classic Stock/H. Armstrong Roberts; p. 161 AF archive/Alamy; p. 162 Chris Mellor/Alamy; p. 163 Oliver Furrer Getty Images; p. 166 Thinkstock/iStock/Anatoliy Fyodorov; p. 168 Picturesbyrob/Alamy; p. 172 Shutterstock.com/Patryk Kosmider; p. 174 Shutterstock.com/Boris Mrdja; p. 176 Thinkstock/iStock/Patricia Marroquin; p. 178 Ersoy Emin/Alamy; p. 180 REX/Red Bull Content Pool; p. 183 NASA